HOLIDAY COOKBOOK

Make holidays throughout the year festive celebrations!

D0568587

INTRODUCTION

Holidays are special days. They're the times you step away from your everyday routines, the times set apart to share with family and friends. Over the years we've helped you plan your holiday celebrations. Now, to make these days even more special, we asked Sylvia Schur, noted food authority, cookbook writer and columnist, to help us create this unique cookbook. It's our way of making holiday cooking part of the fun.

We offer you a year-round collection of thoroughly tested menus and recipes — some for casual times, some for elegant times; some that can be put together quickly, others that call for a bit of advance planning. Whether you're a traditionalist or a trend-setter, a practiced party-giver or beginner, you're sure to find recipes ideal for your holiday plans.

There's an international accent with favorites from around the world, all translated into measures you know and ingredients you probably have on hand. Try Kulich and Paskha, from Russia for Easter; Coeur à la Crème, a French delight for Valentine's Day; Potato Latkes for Hanukkah and a merrie olde English Christmas dinner, featuring Roast Goose and a flaming Plum Pudding. Savor the sophisticated flair of Beef Wellington or Leg of Lamb Persillé, or enjoy the simple pleasure of Cold Herbed Chicken or a Cheese Tray. Add a touch of whimsy with a Shamrock Pie on St. Patrick's Day, an Easter basket made of meringue or Jack-o'-Lantern Burgers for Halloween.

Included, too, are menus for junior cooks, birthday cakes that literally take the cake for kids of all ages plus a hand-picked selection of Christmas gifts that are yours for the making.

But don't stop with our menus and recipes. You'll also find things to do ahead, shopping tips, decorating suggestions and ideas for entertaining.

It's our way of saying "Happy Holidays" — to you, from Hallmark.

Copyright © 1978 by Hallmark Cards, Inc. All rights reserved. Printed in the U.S.A.

TABLE OF CONTENTS

BE A VALENTINE

Create a memory that will be cherished forever with a sentimental celebration on Valentine's Day. Surround yourself with hearts and flowers for an evening filled with love.

To match your Valentine mood, go a bit above and beyond. Here's a menu for two couples made memorable with game hens, a heart-shaped salad and a classic do-in-advance dessert.

CORNISH GAME HENS
WITH BROWN RICE STUFFING
PEAS AND MUSHROOMS BONNE FEMME
AVOCADO WITH CHERRY TOMATOES
COEUR A LA CREME

CORNISH GAME HENS WITH BROWN RICE STUFFING

4   **Cornish game hens (about 1 pound each)**
½   **teaspoon salt (preferably coarse)**
    Pinch of pepper
¼   **teaspoon curry powder**
¼   **teaspoon ground ginger**

STUFFING

1   **tablespoon butter**
2   **shallots, or 1 small white onion and**
      1 clove garlic, minced
¼   **pound fresh mushrooms, sliced lengthwise**
½   **teaspoon curry powder**
½   **cup brown rice**
2   **tablespoons raisins**
1   **cup plus 2 tablespoons chicken broth**
2   **teaspoons grated orange peel**

TO FINISH

2   **tablespoons butter**
2   **tablespoons oil**
¼   **cup dry white wine or apple cider**
    Juice of ½ orange
1   **egg yolk**

Thaw Cornish hens if frozen. Combine salt, pepper, curry and ginger. Rub all over hens to season.

Prepare stuffing: Heat 1 tablespoon butter in a large skillet; stir in shallots and mushrooms and cook briefly, then stir in curry powder. Add rice and sauté over medium heat about 2 minutes. Stir in raisins and broth. Cover skillet and bring to a boil. Reduce heat and simmer about 30 minutes, until rice is almost tender. Add grated orange peel; fluff rice.

Spoon stuffing into cavities of hens, pulling a mushroom slice over the opening. Secure legs, trussing with white thread.

Heat remaining butter and the oil in a large skillet. Add the hens, one at a time, turning to coat and glaze all sides.

Place glazed hens on rack in a roasting pan; baste with wine. Cover loosely with foil and roast in a preheated 375° oven about 30 minutes. Uncover and baste with drippings and orange juice; reduce temperature to 325° and bake another 20 to 30 minutes, until tender and golden. Reduce temperature to 150° and hold until ready to serve.

Just before serving, strain the drippings into a small saucepan. Beat egg yolk with a little of the hot drippings, then return to pan and heat, stirring, to thicken slightly — do not boil.

Place the birds on a large platter. Spoon some of sauce over birds, and garnish with watercress. Serve remaining sauce separately.

4 servings.

NOTE: If desired, before placing the birds on the platter, remove stuffing. Then arrange stuffing around the birds, spoon on sauce and garnish.

PEAS AND MUSHROOMS BONNE FEMME

- 2 tablespoons butter
- 1 small white onion, finely chopped
- ¼ pound fresh mushrooms, sliced, or 1 can (3 ounces) sliced mushrooms
- 3 pounds fresh small peas, shelled, or 1 package (10 ounces) frozen tiny peas, thawed
- 2 tablespoons chicken broth or liquid from canned mushrooms
  Salt and white pepper to taste
  Broad lettuce leaf

In a saucepan or skillet, heat butter and sauté onion and mushrooms about 3 minutes, turning to glaze.

Add peas, broth, salt and pepper. Cover vegetables with broad lettuce leaf, then cover pan. Steam about 4 minutes, shaking pan to cook evenly. Discard leaf before serving.

4 servings.

AVOCADO WITH CHERRY TOMATOES

- 2 ripe avocados
- 1 small head Boston or curly leaf lettuce (optional)
- 12 cherry tomatoes, halved
- ½ cup Hallmark Salad Dressing (page 18)

Use ripe avocados which yield slightly to pressure. (To hasten ripening, place avocados in a brown paper bag.) Shortly before serving, slit the avocado skin lengthwise into fourths; pull back the skin to peel. Cut each avocado lengthwise in half, twisting to release pit. Cut each half into 4 lengthwise slices.

If desired, arrange lettuce leaves on each salad plate. Place 2 pairs of avocado slices, wide ends up, on leaves to form a heart shape. Fill "heart" with cherry tomatoes. Spoon Hallmark Salad Dressing over and serve.

4 servings.

A beautiful finish for a lovely day, at left.

COEUR A LA CREME

- ½ pound cottage cheese
- 1 package (8 ounces) cream cheese, softened
  Pinch of salt
- 1 cup heavy cream
- 1 pint fresh or frozen (thawed) strawberries or raspberries

Sieve cottage cheese or whirl in a blender or food processor. Beat together with cream cheese and salt. Add cream and beat until the mixture is smooth.

Turn the mixture into 4 individual heart-shaped baskets or porcelain coeur dishes lined with moistened cheesecloth (or use 1 large basket or coeur dish). Place each basket over a bowl or place dishes on a platter; refrigerate overnight to drain.

Before serving, turn out of container(s) and garnish with whole berries.

4 servings.

NOTE: Baskets and coeur à la crème molds are readily available in gourmet cookware shops.

6

VALENTINE SPECIALTIES

Start the day right. Even a young Valentine cook can turn hearts with these.

BREAKFAST HEARTS

Cut 6 slices of firm day-old bread into heart shapes with a cookie cutter or knife. In a wide bowl, beat ½ cup milk or light cream with 2 eggs and a pinch of salt until foamy. Drop bread hearts into egg mixture, turning and piercing with a fork to absorb as much mixture as possible.

Heat butter in skillet and brown hearts on both sides. Serve with warmed raspberry syrup.

2 or 3 servings.

An ideal snack to serve with drinks. You'll find it's hard to resist these delicate tidbits.

CHEESE BITES

    2 cups flour
    1 cup butter, slightly softened
    1 cup grated Cheddar cheese
    1 egg, lightly beaten with 1 tablespoon water
       Sesame seeds

Measure flour into a circle in a wide bowl. Inside the circle, cream butter and cheese and work into the flour with a fork. Form into a ball and chill.

Using half the dough at a time, roll between 2 pieces of waxed paper until ⅛ inch thick. Cut into hearts, arrows or other shapes. Brush with beaten egg mixture and sprinkle with sesame seeds. Bake on a chilled baking sheet in a preheated 375° oven about 10 minutes or until golden and firm.

About 4 dozen 2-inch snacks.

Day or night, greet your Valentine visitors with this sure-to-please spread.

HEAVENLY BLUE MOUSSE

    1 pound blue cheese
    2 cups heavy cream
       Thin-sliced pumpernickel bread

Bring blue cheese to room temperature. Beat smooth with a fork, or push through a sieve for extra smoothness. Whip cream until thick and fold into blue cheese.

Butter a 1-quart heart-shaped metal mold and line sides with pumpernickel bread. Pile blue cheese mixture into mold and chill. To serve, slip knife between bread and mold to loosen, then turn out. Serve as a spread with additional slices of pumpernickel bread.

An old-fashioned way to say, "I love you."

SWEETHEART COOKIES

    ¾ cup sweet butter
    ¾ cup sugar
    1 egg yolk
    2 cups flour
    ¼ teaspoon salt
    1 tablespoon lemon juice
       Red decorator's sugar or candy hearts

Cream butter and add sugar gradually, beating until light and fluffy. Beat in egg yolk. Add flour and salt, stirring just to combine. Stir in lemon juice. Gather dough into a ball; if desired, wrap in waxed paper and chill.

Using half the dough at a time, roll out on lightly floured surface until ⅛ inch thick. Cut with a heart-shaped cookie cutter and place on a cold ungreased baking sheet. Sprinkle with decorator's sugar or press a candy heart in center of each. Bake in a preheated 400° oven 6 to 8 minutes or until golden. Cool on baking sheet.

About 4 dozen 2-inch cookies.

Remember these spicy cookies all year long — just change the shape to match the holiday.

SAINT VALENTINE COOKIES

½ cup plus 1 tablespoon brown sugar
⅓ cup heavy cream
¼ cup molasses
½ teaspoon ground ginger
½ teaspoon grated lemon peel
2¼ cups flour
¾ teaspoon baking soda

Beat brown sugar and cream until thick. Add molasses, ginger and lemon peel; mix well. Sift flour with the baking soda and gradually add to creamed mixture. Knead until smooth. Chill several hours or overnight.

On a lightly floured surface, roll out the dough until ⅛ inch thick. Cut with a heart-shaped cookie cutter and place on a lightly greased baking sheet. Bake in a preheated 275° oven 15 minutes. Cool on baking sheet.

If desired, make pink frosting by beating a little berry juice with confectioners' sugar and "paint" or pipe onto cookies.

About 4 dozen 2-inch cookies.

CHOCOLATE-DIPPED STRAWBERRIES

1 quart perfect whole strawberries
8 ounces semisweet chocolate

Wipe berries clean; keep hulls intact.

Grate chocolate into the top of a double boiler and heat over simmering water (water should not touch bottom of pan) until chocolate reaches 110° on a candy thermometer. Remove top of double boiler and continue stirring until chocolate cools to 80°.

To dip berries, hold by the stem and dip each into warm chocolate to cover all but the green hull. Allow excess chocolate to drip off and place berries on waxed paper to set.

NOTE: Be sure to dip berries in a cool place — no warmer than 70°.

CHOCOLATE CHERRY CORDIALS

¼ cup butter, softened
2 cups confectioners' sugar
1 tablespoon light cream or milk
½ teaspoon vanilla
3 drops almond extract
2 jars (6 ounces each) maraschino cherries, drained
1 package (12 ounces) semisweet chocolate bits
1 tablespoon shortening

Cream butter and confectioners' sugar, then add cream, vanilla and almond extract. Using a wooden spoon or an electric mixer at lowest speed, work the mixture until it forms a thick, pliable fondant. If too sticky to shape with the hands, work in a little more confectioners' sugar, ½ tablespoon at a time.

Dry cherries on paper towels. Mold a small amount of fondant (about 1 teaspoon) around each cherry to cover completely. Arrange cherries on a tray, cover lightly with waxed paper or plastic wrap and refrigerate 30 minutes.

Melt chocolate with shortening in the top of a double boiler over hot water; cool, stirring frequently, until thickened and no longer warm to the touch. Drop cherries one at a time into chocolate and turn to cover completely. Remove with a fork and drop onto waxed paper. Chill 15 minutes to harden chocolate. Before serving, store candies in a cool place for 2 days so that the fondant will liquefy.

45 to 50 candies.

 ENTERTAINING IDEAS

To add elegance to your Valentine dinner, place a rose on each napkin. Tie a bow on long stems for the ladies and cut boutonnieres for the men.

For extra fun, hide Valentine cards where they will be discovered throughout the day . . . inside a coat pocket, a lunch box or even the refrigerator.

Need a big table decoration for a children's party? Arrange decorated cupcakes in a heart shape and serve with ice cream as dessert.

SHARIN' OF THE GREEN

Food and merriment toast the wearin' of the green at a traditional St. Patrick's Day feast. With shamrocks for good luck, surely everyone can be a little Irish today.

You can say it's the luck of the Irish that makes this dinner for four so deliciously simple.

GLAZED CORNED BEEF
PARSLEYED NEW POTATOES
KILLARNEY COLESLAW
IRISH SODA BREAD
SHAMROCK PIE   IRISH COFFEE

GLAZED CORNED BEEF

  3 pounds corned beef
  1 clove garlic
  1 bay leaf
  4 peppercorns
  ¼ cup apple juice
  ⅓ cup brown sugar
  2 teaspoons prepared mustard

Place corned beef in a large saucepan and cover with cold water. Add garlic, bay leaf and peppercorns. Cover and bring to a boil. Reduce heat and simmer about 3 hours or until tender.

Remove corned beef from liquid and place fat-side up on a rack in a roasting pan. Score the fat in a diamond pattern.

Prepare the glaze by combining apple juice, brown sugar and mustard in a small saucepan. Stir over low heat until well blended and slightly thickened. Pour glaze over meat. Roast in a preheated 400° oven 30 minutes, basting every 10 minutes to glaze.

4 to 6 servings (with leftovers).

NOTE: The leftovers are great for sandwiches.

PARSLEYED NEW POTATOES

  1½ pounds new potatoes
  ½ teaspoon salt
  ¼ cup butter
  2 tablespoons chopped parsley

Scrub potatoes to remove any loose skin. Pare a ½-inch strip around the center of each potato to prevent splitting. In a saucepan, bring about 2 inches water to a boil. Add salt and potatoes. Cover and boil about 20 minutes or until tender. Uncover and quickly boil off remaining water, shaking the pan to dry potatoes. Add butter, in pieces, and parsley, turning potatoes to coat evenly.

4 servings.

KILLARNEY COLESLAW

  3 cups shredded cabbage
  ½ green pepper, shredded
  2 tablespoons grated onion
  ¾ teaspoon salt
  ¼ teaspoon pepper
  ½ teaspoon celery seeds
  1 tablespoon sugar
  ¾ cup mayonnaise
  1 tablespoon lemon juice
  2 tablespoons chopped fresh parsley
  1 teaspoon chopped chives

Combine cabbage, green pepper, onion, salt, pepper, celery seeds and sugar. Whirl remaining ingredients in a blender (or whip with a fork). Combine and toss well. Refrigerate until ready to serve.

4 servings.

IRISH SODA BREAD

4 cups flour
1 tablespoon baking powder
1 teaspoon salt
½ teaspoon baking soda
1 cup raisins
1 tablespoon caraway seeds
2 cups buttermilk

In a bowl, sift together flour, baking powder, salt and baking soda. Add raisins and caraway seeds; stir well. Stir in buttermilk to make a soft dough.

Knead the dough very lightly and divide in half. Shape each half into a round loaf and place on a greased baking sheet. Bake in a preheated 375° oven 45 minutes or until golden.

2 small loaves.

NOTE: Freeze the extra loaf, or better yet, gift-wrap it as a special St. Patrick's Day greeting.

SHAMROCK PIE

Chocolate Shamrocks (below)
1 cup chocolate wafer crumbs
¼ cup butter, softened
1 package (3 ounces) lime-flavored gelatin
½ cup boiling water
1 pint vanilla or pistachio ice cream, softened

Prepare Chocolate Shamrocks and refrigerate. Combine crumbs and softened butter. Press against bottom and sides of an 8-inch pie plate.

Empty gelatin into a bowl; add boiling water and stir to dissolve. Stir in ice cream a few spoonfuls at a time, beating vigorously as it thickens. Pile mixture into the lined pie plate and chill until serving time. Place shamrocks on pie.

CHOCOLATE SHAMROCKS

Melt 4 ounces semisweet chocolate over hot water; spread evenly on a sheet of waxed paper. Let cool until firm. Press a lightly oiled shamrock-shaped cookie cutter sharply into chocolate (or cut around a shamrock pattern). Leave shamrocks on the waxed paper and refrigerate until ready to use.

IRISH COFFEE

4 tablespoons sugar
4 ounces Irish whiskey
4 cups freshly brewed strong coffee
1 cup whipped cream

Set out 4 Irish coffee glasses and dissolve 1 tablespoon sugar in 1 ounce of whiskey in each glass. Fill to ½ inch from the rim with hot strong coffee; float whipped cream on top.

4 servings.

☘ ENTERTAINING IDEAS

Whether you're entertaining friends or the family, a centerpiece adds holiday flair to your table. For an informal gathering, fill a small basket with Irish potatoes and broccoli accented with a green bow. To add a St. Patrick's touch to a bouquet of fresh flowers, place Hallmark St. Patrick's Day seals back-to-back on lengths of florist's wire. The seals add a sprinkling of shamrocks to any arrangement.

On St. Patrick's Day everyone wants to be a little bit Irish. Greet guests to your St. Patrick's Day party with a hand-lettered sign on the door: "Welcome to the O'Smiths'" (or whatever your last name is).

Make sure all your guests are ready for the Wearin' of the Green with Hallmark lapel pins or cloth buttons. Give one to each guest wearing green and have some shamrock silhouettes to pin on guests who arrive "greenless."

There's nothing like an Irish songfest for keeping your guests in a happy mood. Include old favorites such as "When Irish Eyes are Smiling," "Peg o' My Heart" and others. Record the music for an amusing play-back later in the evening.

If you want to include a game, see how many words each guest can make out of "leprechaun," "shillelagh" or "blarney." Paint small rocks green before the party and award pieces of the "Blarney Stone" to the contest winners.

SPRINGTIME SPECIALTIES

Welcome springtime with a parade of exciting Easter treats. From a picture-perfect brunch to surprising specialties, it's a delicious way to celebrate the coming of spring.

Be prepared for the Easter parade to end at your house with a buffet brunch featuring holiday favorites from around the world. Greet your guests with a refreshing eggnog, then direct them to the buffet centered with a command-performance Easter ham.

ORANGE EGGNOG
EASTER HAM
HERB-SCRAMBLED EGGS
KULICH   PASKHA

ORANGE EGGNOG

  4 eggs, separated
 ½ cup sugar
  1 cup bourbon (optional)
 ¼ cup orange liqueur (optional)
 ½ teaspoon finely grated orange peel
  1 cup freshly squeezed orange juice
  1 cup heavy cream
 ½ cup light cream
    Freshly grated nutmeg

Beat egg yolks and sugar until thick. Beat in bourbon and liqueur. Stir in orange peel and orange juice, then stir in heavy cream and light cream.

Beat egg whites until stiff but not dry; fold into the orange juice mixture. Pour into a chilled punch bowl and sprinkle nutmeg over the top.

12 servings (3 ounces each).

NOTE: For family service, combine eggnog ingredients without the bourbon and liqueur; stir into each individual serving as desired (about ⅔ ounce bourbon and a dash of the liqueur).

EASTER HAM

 ½ fully cooked ham (5 to 6 pounds)
  1 cup pineapple juice
 ¾ cup light brown sugar
  2 teaspoons dry mustard
 ½ teaspoon ground ginger
  1 can (10 ounces) mandarin orange sections,
     drained
    Whole cloves

Prepare ham for baking as directed on label. (For extra succulence, bring ham to a boil in a large saucepan of water; drain.) Place ham on a rack in a roasting pan and bake in a preheated 325° oven 1 hour. Remove from oven and, with a knife, score fat in a scallop pattern.

Combine pineapple juice, sugar, mustard and ginger in a small saucepan. Bring to a boil and cook, stirring, until slightly thickened. Baste ham with some of juice mixture. Increase oven temperature to 425° and bake ham for 10 minutes. Remove from oven and center a mandarin orange section in each scallop, securing with a clove. Brush ham all over with juice mixture and bake 20 minutes longer, basting frequently.

6 to 8 servings (with leftovers).

NOTE: For a tangy sauce to complement the flavor of the ham, heat the remaining glazing sauce with 2 teaspoons cider vinegar, 1 teaspoon Worcestershire sauce and any remaining mandarin orange segments. Pour into a sauceboat and serve with the ham.

HERB-SCRAMBLED EGGS

    8 to 12 eggs
    ½ to ¾ cup light cream
    ½ teaspoon salt
       Pinch of pepper
    2 to 3 tablespoons chopped fresh herbs
       (parsley, chives, tarragon) or 1 tablespoon
       dried mixed herbs
    ¼ cup butter

Beat eggs with cream, salt, pepper and herbs. In a large skillet, heat butter until bubbling (do not let butter brown); pour in egg mixture. Cook over low heat, using a spatula to stir set portions of egg in from the sides — do not overcook.

6 to 8 servings.

NOTE: Let the youngsters "blow out" the eggs and use the shells to make Jellied Easter "Eggs" (page 19). Add them to the menu if you like.

KULICH

    2 packages active dry yeast
    ½ cup warm water
    ½ cup warm milk
    6½ cups flour
    4 eggs plus 2 yolks, beaten
    1 cup butter, melted
    ½ cup raisins
    ½ teaspoon vanilla
    ½ cup honey
    ½ teaspoon salt
    1 cup sugar
    2 tablespoons salad oil
       Confectioners' Sugar Glaze (right)

Dissolve yeast in warm water in a large bowl. Add milk and 1½ cups of the flour; stir until smooth. Cover and let rise in a warm place until doubled in bulk, 3 hours or more. Beat down dough. Add remaining ingredients except Confectioners' Sugar Glaze, beating in remaining flour gradually. Knead in bowl until dough is smooth and elastic.

For the baking pans, use 2 tall 1-pound coffee cans. Grease pans and fit each one with a collar of greased brown paper (this will add height to the bread). Fill pans ⅔ full of dough. Cover and let rise in a warm place until doubled in bulk, at least 1 hour.

Bake in a preheated 375° oven about 1 hour or until well browned. Cool in cans 10 minutes, then remove to a rack. When cool, spread with Confectioners' Sugar Glaze, allowing some to drizzle down the sides.

CONFECTIONERS' SUGAR GLAZE

    1 cup confectioners' sugar
    ½ teaspoon vanilla
    4 teaspoons heavy cream

Combine all ingredients and beat until smooth.

NOTE: Kulich and Paskha are traditional Russian Easter foods. For easy buffet service, remove the cap from the Kulich and cut the bread crosswise into rounds. Re-form and top with the cap. Each person takes a bread round and spreads it with Paskha.

PASKHA

    2 pounds cottage cheese
    2 hard-boiled eggs
    ½ cup butter, softened
    1 package (3 ounces) cream cheese
    ¼ cup confectioners' sugar
    ½ cup raisins
    ½ cup ground almonds
    ½ cup chopped candied fruits: orange peel,
       lemon peel, cherries

Sieve cottage cheese and hard-boiled eggs together. Beat in butter and cream cheese, then beat in sugar. Add raisins, ground almonds and candied fruits.

Press mixture into a new 6-inch flowerpot (or use any container that provides drainage) lined with cheesecloth. Place in a bowl and allow to drain overnight in the refrigerator. Unmold to serve. If desired, garnish with additional candied fruits.

8 or more servings.

NOTE: You'll find that Paskha can stand on its own as a dinner dessert. The Orthodox Russians make it in special wooden forms, but these are not commonly available.

1. The paper collar around the coffee can adds height to the Kulich.

2. The cheesecloth lining allows the Paskha mixture to drain but prevents it from slipping out. It also makes the unmolding easier.

3. Paskha and Kulich, the traditional pairing of Russian Easter fare.

Bring on the colors of spring with a special Easter dinner that takes an inspired approach to traditional favorites. Complement leg of lamb with garden-fresh vegetables and a delightful springtime dessert.

FRESH ASPARAGUS WITH HOLLANDAISE SAUCE
LEG OF LAMB PERSILLE
NOODLE BAKE
SPRING GREEN SALAD
WITH HALLMARK SALAD DRESSING
DAFFODIL SHORTCAKE

FRESH ASPARAGUS WITH HOLLANDAISE SAUCE

3 pounds asparagus
½ teaspoon salt
Hollandaise Sauce (below)
Pimiento strips (optional)

Snap off tough ends from asparagus stalks. Scrub the asparagus; if stalks are thick, scrape bottom sections with a vegetable scraper. Bring 2 cups water to a boil in a deep saucepan. Stand asparagus upright in boiling water. Cover (you may have to use an inverted saucepan) and steam just until tender, about 12 minutes. Drain carefully and keep warm, covered with a kitchen towel.

Prepare Hollandaise Sauce. Arrange asparagus on salad plates for the first course. Spoon sauce over spears. Garnish each serving with crossed strips of pimiento.

6 to 8 servings.

HOLLANDAISE SAUCE

½ cup (1 stick) butter, chilled
3 egg yolks
1 tablespoon lemon juice
Pinch of salt

Place chilled butter in a cold heavy 6-inch saucepan. Add egg yolks, lemon juice and salt. Stir over *low heat* until butter melts and combines with yolks and juice. Stir another minute until sauce thickens.

NOTE: If sauce should curdle, remove from heat and beat in 1 tablespoon boiling water until smooth.

LEG OF LAMB PERSILLE

1 leg of lamb (5 to 6 pounds)
2 cloves garlic, crushed (optional)
Salt and pepper
3 tablespoons lemon juice or vinegar
4 cups fresh bread crumbs
1 cup finely chopped fresh parsley
1 teaspoon thyme
¾ cup butter, melted
Fresh parsley sprigs

Ask your butcher to trim the fell (the thin outer covering) from lamb leg. Rub lamb with garlic and season with salt and pepper. Sprinkle with lemon juice. (The juice will season the lamb and lessen the cooking aroma.)

Combine bread crumbs, chopped parsley and thyme with melted butter and set aside until 30 minutes before roast is done.

Roast lamb uncovered in a preheated 325° oven, allowing 25 minutes per pound for rare, 30 minutes for medium and 34 minutes for well done. Remove lamb from oven about 30 minutes before it is done and press parsley-crumb mixture firmly on top and sides of leg, covering completely. Return lamb to oven and roast 30 minutes longer, until coating turns golden. Garnish with parsley sprigs.

6 to 8 servings.

NOODLE BAKE

1 package (16 ounces) egg noodles
¾ cup grated cheese (Gruyère, Cheddar, Swiss)
4 eggs
1 cup milk
¼ teaspoon salt
Pinch of pepper

Cook noodles according to package directions; drain well. Toss noodles lightly with grated cheese, reserving 2 tablespoons for topping. Place noodles in a buttered casserole. Beat eggs lightly; add milk, salt and pepper and pour over noodles. Sprinkle top with reserved cheese. Bake uncovered in a preheated 325° oven 45 minutes or until thickened.

6 to 8 servings.

SPRING GREEN SALAD WITH HALLMARK SALAD DRESSING

1 large bunch watercress
2 or 3 heads Boston lettuce
  Hallmark Salad Dressing (below)

Before untying watercress, cut off and discard about 1 inch of stems. Separate lettuce into leaves. Wash watercress and lettuce leaves in ice-cold water; dry well and chill. Meanwhile, prepare Hallmark Salad Dressing. When ready to serve, arrange lettuce leaves on individual salad plates or in small salad bowls and top with watercress. Serve the dressing on the side.

6 to 8 servings.

NOTE: If you prefer, the greens and dressing (about ¼ cup) can be tossed in a large salad bowl. For a special Easter touch, tuck a Tulip Egg garnish into the bowl. Cut off the top of a hard-boiled egg. Using a small sharp knife, cut a zigzag edge into the remaining portion. If desired, brush a little food coloring or beet juice onto the egg white.

HALLMARK SALAD DRESSING

2 tablespoons cider vinegar
1 tablespoon lemon juice
1 egg
½ teaspoon salt
⅛ teaspoon paprika
½ teaspoon dry mustard
½ teaspoon crushed herbs (tarragon, chervil, parsley, marjoram)
  Freshly ground pepper
  Pinch of cayenne pepper
1 cup salad oil

In a small bowl, whisk together vinegar, lemon juice, egg and seasonings. Gradually whisk in oil until dressing is light and emulsified but still pourable. Refrigerate until ready to serve. (The dressing can be stored, tightly covered, in the refrigerator for up to 5 days.)

About 1⅓ cups.

DAFFODIL SHORTCAKE

6 eggs, separated
½ teaspoon cream of tartar
½ teaspoon vanilla
1½ cups granulated sugar
1¼ cups flour
¼ teaspoon salt
1 teaspoon baking powder
¼ cup cold water
2 teaspoons lemon juice
1 teaspoon grated lemon peel
1 cup heavy cream
1 tablespoon confectioners' sugar
1 quart fresh strawberries, washed and hulled

Beat egg whites until foamy. Add cream of tartar and beat until soft, moist peaks form. Add vanilla. Fold in ¾ cup of the granulated sugar, about 2 tablespoons at a time. Sift ½ cup of the flour with ⅛ teaspoon of the salt. Fold into egg whites, sifting in about ¼ cup at a time.

Beat egg yolks about 3 minutes. Gradually beat in the remaining ¾ cup granulated sugar. Sift the remaining ¾ cup flour with baking powder and the remaining ⅛ teaspoon salt. Beat flour into yolk mixture alternately with cold water, lemon juice and peel.

Alternating white and yellow mixtures, spoon the 2 batters into an ungreased 10-inch tube pan. Bake in a preheated 325° oven about 50 minutes. Invert pan, slipping center tube over a soda bottle so that the cake does not rest directly on a surface. Cool completely, then remove from pan.

Just before serving, beat heavy cream with confectioners' sugar until stiff peaks form. Cut cake into individual serving pieces; top with whipped cream and berries.

NOTE: Adapt the fruit topping on the shortcake to match your taste preferences or the season. Instead of strawberries, try blueberries, raspberries, seedless grapes, melon balls, sliced bananas, peaches or pears. If using canned or frozen fruit, be sure to drain thoroughly.

EASTER SPECIALTIES

What to do with all those decorated eggs? Here's an unusual day-after disguise.

ELEGANT DEVILED EGGS

 8 hard-boiled eggs
¼ cup mayonnaise
 2 tablespoons sour cream
 1 tablespoon prepared mustard
 1 jar (about 2 ounces) red caviar

Remove shells from eggs and cut eggs lengthwise in half. Carefully remove yolks and mash with mayonnaise, sour cream and mustard. Pile mixture into egg whites and garnish with red caviar.

8 servings.

If you're scrambling eggs for breakfast, don't just crack them. Use the shells for this gelatin surprise.

JELLIED EASTER "EGGS"

 2 packages (3 ounces each) fruit-flavored gelatin
 3 cups hot water
12 eggs

Prepare gelatin as directed, using only 1½ cups hot water for each package. (Use two different flavors for color variety.) Chill until slightly thickened.

Using a darning needle or a small skewer, puncture a small hole in the narrow end of each egg; puncture a wider hole in the broader end. Hold egg over bowl and put lips to the smaller hole; gently blow egg out of the shell into the bowl. Repeat with each egg. Wash shells gently with cold water. Blow all water out of shells. Light a candle and hold over the smaller hole of each shell, allowing the melting wax to drip over it to seal. Set aside to harden.

Pour slightly thickened gelatin into empty egg shells, using a small spoon or funnel. Set shells upright in carton and refrigerate at least 3 hours to set. To remove "eggs," crack shells by rolling on a table and peel gently, wetting hands to handle gelatin. Refrigerate until serving time. To serve, arrange on lettuce leaves or a nest of shredded carrots.

A holiday fruit bread that comes in two guises — with almonds for Easter, without for Christmas.

PANETTONE

 2 packages active dry yeast
1½ cups sugar
½ cup warm water
 1 cup butter, softened
 7 eggs, lightly beaten
½ cup warm milk
 6 cups flour
½ teaspoon salt
 1 cup golden seedless raisins
¾ cup chopped candied citron
½ cup blanched slivered almonds
 1 egg yolk
   Light cream

Combine yeast, ¼ cup of the sugar and warm water. Stir to dissolve. In a large bowl, cream butter with remaining sugar. Beat eggs into the butter-sugar mixture, then beat in yeast mixture and milk. Sift in flour and salt and beat well. Add raisins, citron and almonds and continue to beat until dough is smooth and satiny.

Grease and flour a 9-inch layer cake pan. Make a 9-inch-high collar of brown paper about 2 or 3 inches longer than the circumference of the pan; grease one side. Fit the collar inside the pan, greased side in, and fasten the top edges with paper clips if necessary. Turn dough into the prepared pan and let rise in a warm place about 4 hours (or in the refrigerator overnight), until more than doubled in height.

Bake in a preheated 350° oven about 1 hour or until well browned. At the halfway point, mix the egg yolk with a little cream and brush on top. Cool, still in the paper collar, on a wire rack.

NOTE: Like other yeast breads, Panettone takes well to freezing. Cool completely after baking, then wrap in moisture-proof freezer paper. (Properly wrapped, yeast breads can be stored in the freezer for about 9 months to a year.) To thaw, let stand at room temperature; do not unwrap. It will take about 3 hours for a loaf this size to thaw completely.

MERINGUE BERRY BASKET

- 6 egg whites (¾ cup)
- ½ teaspoon cream of tartar
- 1¼ cups granulated sugar
- ½ cup confectioners' sugar
- Fresh whole strawberries
- Whipped cream

Cover 2 baking sheets with unglazed brown paper. On one, draw an 8-inch circle and 2 matching curves, each about 8 inches across at the open ends and about 4 inches high. (After baking, the curves will be joined to form the basket handle.) On the second sheet of paper, draw two 8-inch circles.

Warm egg whites slightly by placing the bowl in warm water. Add cream of tartar and beat until stiff but not dry. Sift sugars together to combine; gradually add to the egg whites, beating until stiff.

Spoon the meringue into a pastry bag fitted with a ½-inch round tip. Pipe the meringue onto the single outlined circle, making a solid base; build up the edge to about 1 inch in height. Pipe the meringue onto the 2 curves that will form the basket handle. On the second tray, pipe the meringue onto the outlines of the circles, forming 2 rings. Each ring should be at least ½ inch high. Reserve a little of the meringue in the bag.

Bake in a 190° oven (or even lower, if possible) until the meringue shapes are dry and can be lifted from the paper easily — about 1½ hours for the rings and curves, 2½ hours for the base. Turn off oven and let base dry in oven 15 minutes longer. Remove and cool.

Place meringue base on a serving plate and "cement" one of the rings to it with some of the remaining meringue; "cement" second ring to the first. Seal the handle halves, flat sides together, with dabs of meringue; set aside until basket is filled.

Fill basket with strawberries and set the handle in place, securing it with the last of the meringue. Serve with a bowl of whipped cream.

NOTE: The basket may be prepared a day or so in advance; store, loosely covered, in a dry place. It may be filled with other berries or fruits or even with a creamy pudding.

COCONUT MARSHMALLOWS

- 1 envelope unflavored gelatin
- ⅓ cup cold water
- ½ cup sugar
- ⅔ cup corn syrup
- ½ teaspoon vanilla
- 2 cups flaked coconut

Sprinkle gelatin on water in the top of a double boiler to soften. Place over boiling water until dissolved. Add sugar and stir to dissolve. Pour into a mixing bowl. Add corn syrup and vanilla. Beat with an electric mixer until thick and light, about 10 minutes. Cover the bottom of an 8-inch square pan with ¾ cup of the coconut. Pour in marshmallow mixture and smooth top. Sprinkle with about ½ cup more coconut. Let stand in a cool place until set, about 1 hour. Loosen edges and turn out onto a board. Cut into 1-inch squares with a knife dipped in cold water; roll cut sides in remaining coconut.

64 marshmallows.

 ENTERTAINING IDEAS

Spring flowers and decorated eggs add a colorful touch to Easter parties. For an Easter brunch or dinner, decorate your table with pastel candles, spring flowers and coordinating paper accessories. If you're serving buffet-style, wrap silverware in individual napkins and tie with a yarn bow.

For an Easter egg hunt with a twist, plan a cookie hunt for the children. Bake cookies in Easter shapes using Hallmark cookie cutters and wrap the cookies individually with cellophane.

Children also can have fun with a "Fill the Easter Basket" game. The host begins by saying, "In my Easter basket, I'm going to put _____," and mentions any item. The next player repeats the phrase including the mentioned item, and adds a new item in the basket. So it goes around the circle with each player repeating all that went before and adding a new item. When a player forgets an item, he is out of the game. The last player left wins.

ESPECIALLY FOR MOM

Today's the day to do something special for Mom.
Pamper her with affection and treat her to a luscious dinner.
It's easier than you think, and fun to do.

Mum's the word when you make this dinner a special Mother's Day surprise. It's as easy as A, B, C if you plan ahead, work together and follow the recipes exactly. You'll find suggested Timing Tips on page 24 and some helpful hints on pages 28-29.

TOMATO-POPCORN SOUP
LAYERED SALMON MOUSSE
SPINACH SALAD
WITH HALLMARK SALAD DRESSING
SESAME BISCUITS
COCOA FLUFF ICEBOX CAKE

TOMATO-POPCORN SOUP

  2 cans (10¾ ounces each) condensed tomato
     soup
1½ soup cans water
 ¼ cup heavy cream
    Ground nutmeg
    Cheese Popcorn (below)

Combine soup and water in a saucepan. Heat, stirring occasionally. Pour the soup into soup bowls or mugs. Swirl a spoonful of cream into each bowl of soup; sprinkle with nutmeg and top with popcorn. Pass the rest of the popcorn for nibbling.

4 servings.

CHEESE POPCORN

 4 cups popped popcorn
 ¼ cup butter, melted
 ¼ cup grated Parmesan cheese

Place popcorn in a deep bowl. Add melted butter and cheese. Toss to coat popcorn thoroughly.

LAYERED SALMON MOUSSE

SALMON LAYER

 1 can (16 ounces) salmon
 1 envelope unflavored gelatin
 ½ cup boiling water
 2 tablespoons lemon juice
 ¼ cup grated onion (optional)
 ½ cup mayonnaise
 1 teaspoon dill weed
 1 cup heavy cream

SALAD LAYER

  1 envelope unflavored gelatin
  ¼ cup sugar
  ½ teaspoon salt
1¼ cups boiling water
  ¼ cup vinegar
  1 tablespoon lime juice
  ½ cup shredded green pepper
  1 cup chopped celery
  1 pimiento, cut into strips

To prepare salmon layer, drain salmon, reserving ¼ cup liquid in a bowl. Sprinkle 1 envelope gelatin on liquid to soften. Add boiling water, stirring to dissolve. Stir in lemon juice and onion. Place salmon in a bowl and remove skin and bones. Flake the fish; add mayonnaise and dill. Add gelatin mixture and beat until smooth. Slowly beat in cream. Pour into an oiled 6-cup mold. Chill in refrigerator.

To prepare salad layer, mix 1 envelope gelatin with sugar and salt. Add boiling water and stir until gelatin is dissolved. Stir in vinegar and lime juice. Chill 20 minutes. Fold in green pepper, celery and pimiento. Spoon over salmon in mold. Chill at least 2 hours. To serve, unmold (see page 29 for unmolding tips); garnish with salad greens and lemon slices.

4 servings.

SPINACH SALAD

Hallmark Salad Dressing (page 18)
1 **package (10 ounces) fresh spinach**
2 **slices bacon, cooked and crumbled (optional)**

Prepare Hallmark Salad Dressing and refrigerate.

Remove stems from spinach leaves. Drop leaves into a bowl of cold water. Swish them around gently, then drop into another bowl of water. Repeat until no sand is left in the water. Pat leaves dry with paper towels. Heap into a salad bowl. Top with crumbled bacon. Toss with the salad dressing.

4 servings.

SESAME BISCUITS

1 **package refrigerated biscuits**
1 **egg**
2 **tablespoons sesame seeds**

Following package directions, separate the biscuits and arrange on a baking sheet. Beat the egg with a fork and brush on biscuits. Sprinkle with sesame seeds. Bake according to package directions.

10 biscuits.

COCOA FLUFF ICEBOX CAKE

24 **ladyfingers**
¼ **cup raspberry or strawberry jelly**
1 **tablespoon hot water**
1½ **cups heavy cream**
⅓ **cup confectioners' sugar**
3 **tablespoons cocoa powder**

Circle the sides and cover the bottom of an attractive bowl (about 6 cups) with ladyfingers. Mix jelly and hot water and drizzle over ladyfingers.

Measure 1½ cups cream, the confectioners' sugar and cocoa into a bowl. Beat with a hand beater until mixture is thick. Heap over ladyfingers in bowl. Refrigerate until ready to serve, at least 30 minutes. If you like, just before serving, beat ½ cup heavy cream and 1 tablespoon granulated sugar until stiff. Spoon onto each serving.

4 to 6 servings.

 TIMING TIPS

It's important to plan ahead for any dinner. Make sure you have all the ingredients on hand before you start. Decide which dishes take the longest to prepare or which ones can be made in advance and refrigerated, and start those first.

It's a good idea to divide the work. Younger cooks can trim and wash the spinach, make the soup and help with the cake while older cooks concentrate on the salmon mousse or cook the bacon for the salad.

Look over the following timetable and adapt it to your own plans for Mother's Day.

In the morning:
• Make salmon mousse and refrigerate.
• Make salad dressing and refrigerate.
• Trim and wash spinach. Dry and wrap in a clean kitchen towel; refrigerate.
• Make icebox cake and refrigerate.

1 hour before dinner:
• Unmold the mousse (see page 29) and refrigerate until ready to serve.
• Set table.

45 minutes before dinner:
• Cook bacon for the salad; drain and crumble.
• Arrange biscuits on baking sheet; brush with egg and top with sesame seeds.

15 minutes before dinner:
• Make soup.
• Put biscuits in oven or toaster oven.

10 minutes before dinner:
• Make popcorn garnish for soup.
• Toss salad.
• Garnish mousse.

Dinnertime:
• Everything is ready!

HOORAY FOR DAD

Here's your once-a-year chance to stir up a surprise that's just for Dad. There's no more loving way to say, "You're our candidate for Father of the Year"... every year.

Especially for junior cooks—here's a hearty dinner designed to suit Dad's tastes. Do as much as you can in advance (see the Timing Tips on page 26) so you can spend time with Dad on his special day.

CRISP VEGETABLES
WITH HERB SOUR CREAM DIP
GOOD CHILI AND TRIMMINGS
BACON UPSIDE-DOWN CORN BREAD
INSTANT "CHEESECAKE"

CRISP VEGETABLES WITH HERB SOUR CREAM DIP

DIP
- ½ cup cottage cheese
- 1 tablespoon lemon juice
  Dash of hot pepper sauce
- 1 green onion, finely chopped, or 2 teaspoons frozen chopped chives
- ¼ teaspoon dried dill weed
  Pinch of garlic powder
- ¼ cup sour cream

VEGETABLES
- 2 medium carrots
- 2 stalks celery, without leaves
- 1 small cucumber
- 1 small zucchini
- 1 green pepper

Combine cottage cheese, lemon juice and hot pepper sauce in a mixing bowl. Beat until smooth. (Or, if you have permission, whirl in a blender.) Stir in green onion, dill, garlic powder and sour cream. Refrigerate at least 1 hour before serving.

Wash all vegetables. Cut carrots, celery, cucumber and zucchini crosswise in half; then cut each half into sticks (about 3 inches long). Cut pepper lengthwise in half and scrape out seeds; cut into strips. Place vegetables in a bowl of ice water and refrigerate (to make them really crispy.) To serve, arrange vegetables on a small tray; place dip bowl in the center.

4 to 6 servings.

GOOD CHILI AND TRIMMINGS

- 1 pound ground beef
- 1 medium onion, finely chopped
- 1 small green pepper, seeded and finely chopped
- ⅛ teaspoon garlic powder or 1 clove garlic, crushed
- 2 tablespoons chili powder
- ½ teaspoon crushed red pepper
- 1½ teaspoons salt
- 1 teaspoon pepper
- 1 can (16 ounces) tomatoes
- 1 can (16 ounces) red kidney beans, drained
  Trimmings (below)

Cook beef in a deep skillet until brown, stirring to break up beef and to cook evenly. Carefully drain fat from skillet.

Add onion, green pepper, garlic powder, chili powder, red pepper, salt and pepper to meat in skillet. Stir. Add tomatoes and kidney beans. Simmer about 20 minutes, stirring frequently, until slightly thickened. Serve in wide soup bowls.

4 servings.

TRIMMINGS

Set out a choice of "trimmings" to be added to the chili: crisp crackers, corn chips, grated cheddar cheese, tomato wedges, green pepper rings.

BACON UPSIDE-DOWN CORN BREAD

1 cup flour
1 cup cornmeal
4 teaspoons baking powder
2 tablespoons sugar
1 teaspoon salt
1 egg
1 cup milk
2 tablespoons butter, melted
12 slices bacon

Place flour, cornmeal, baking powder, sugar and salt in a bowl and toss to mix. Beat egg with a fork or hand beater; add to flour mixture. Then add the milk and melted butter. Stir until mixture is thoroughly moistened — do not overmix.

Fry bacon slices until partially cooked. (The bacon should be limp — not crisp.) Drain on paper towels. Line the bottom of a very lightly greased 9-inch square baking pan with waxed paper. Arrange bacon slices on the waxed paper and along sides of pan. Pour batter into bacon-lined pan. Bake in a preheated 400° oven about 30 minutes or until well browned.

Remove pan from oven and allow to cool a few minutes. Turn bread out of pan upside-down on a board — the bacon will be on top. Remove waxed paper and cut bread into squares. Serve warm.

INSTANT "CHEESECAKE"

1 cup graham cracker crumbs
2 tablespoons sugar
¼ cup butter, melted
¾ cup milk
1 cup sour cream
1 package (3¾ ounces) vanilla instant pudding

Combine cracker crumbs, sugar and melted butter in a bowl and mix well. Pour crumb mixture into an 8-inch pie plate; press firmly and evenly against bottom and sides of plate to form the crust.

Combine milk and sour cream in a mixing bowl. Add instant pudding. Beat with a hand beater *just* until smooth, about 1 minute. Pour into the pie crust. Chill until set, at least 2 hours.

 TIMING TIPS

Doing as much as you can in advance is the key to having any dinner ready on time, with no last-minute rush. Look over the following suggested timetable and adapt it to your plans for the day. Almost everything, with the exception of the corn bread, can be done ahead of time. So if Dad wants to go to the ball game or watch one on television, you'll be free to join him.

The day before:
• Make cheesecake; refrigerate.
• Make dip; refrigerate.

2 hours before dinner:
• Partially cook bacon slices for corn bread; arrange bacon slices in baking pan as directed.
• Wash and cut fresh vegetables for dipping; refrigerate in a bowl of ice water. (This can also be done early in the day.)
• Set table.

1½ hours before dinner:
• Make chili. Let simmer slowly. When chili is done, turn off heat; reheat just before dinnertime. (If you prefer, the chili can be made early in the day or even the day before. Cover and refrigerate. Reheat about 10 minutes.)

1 hour before dinner:
• Mix batter for corn bread.

40 minutes before dinner:
• Put corn bread in oven.
• Arrange "trimmings" for chili in bowls.

10 minutes before dinner:
• Remove corn bread from oven to turn out onto board.
• Get vegetables and dip ready for serving.
• If necessary, reheat chili.

Dinnertime:
• Everything is ready!

The more you know about cooking, the more fun it will be.

1. When using a knife or grater, be sure the fingers of your hand holding the food are turned in.

2. Spinach is very sandy. Swish it around in lots of water, then drain on paper towels.

3. Cream will whip faster if the beater, the bowl and the cream are all chilled.

4. Dip a mold into hot water just to loosen. Top with a plate and turn both over. If the food doesn't unmold, dip again.

5. Always measure liquids on a level surface. Read the measurement at eye level.

6. If you roll out crumbs between two sheets of waxed paper, you can pick them up easily.

TIPS FOR JUNIOR COOKS

When it's time to remember your favorite people, a great way to do it is to cook up your own personal surprise. But to make sure the surprise isn't on you, here are some rules that all good cooks follow.

Be Smart Before You Start
• Read through each recipe you're going to make, and be sure you understand it. Check that you have all the ingredients and equipment you need.
• Make a clean sweep of it. Tie back extra-long hair. Put on your apron and scrub your hands and nails. While you're at it, wash off working surfaces.
• Get out all the ingredients for the recipes you are making and put them on a tray. Put them back where they belong as you use them — that way you'll know you haven't forgotten to add anything. Get out all the utensils you'll need.
• Baking has special rules. Unless the recipe says otherwise, have ingredients at room temperature.

Measuring Up
• A recipe is only as good as its measurements — if they're off, the recipe will be, too. Always use standard marked cups and spoons for measuring. Cups and spoons used for drinking and eating won't do.
• The following table of equivalent measurements will come in handy.

    3 teaspoons = 1 tablespoon
    4 tablespoons = ¼ cup
    5 tablespoons plus 1 teaspoon = ⅓ cup
    8 tablespoons = ½ cup
    1 cup = ½ pint
    2 cups = 1 pint
    4 cups = 1 quart

Sharp Thinking
• Dull knives are dangerous. You have to push to make them cut. When you push, the knife may slip and cut your finger instead of the food.
• Sharp knives are dangerous, too, if you leave them lying around. Never leave them in a sink of soapy water where they can't be seen, or on a counter where they can accidentally fall.
• When slicing, keep the fingers of your hand holding the food curled back. When chopping, hold the tip of the knife against the board and rock the handle up and down to chop the food. Use a vegetable peeler to peel fruits and vegetables.

• When using a grater or shredder, again keep your fingers holding the food curled in.

When the Heat's On
• Use the oven only if you have permission to do so.
• Removing food from the oven or stove top can be tricky. Everything's hot — the door, the racks, the dish, the handles, the food. Use pot holders, and try it only if you have permission. Otherwise, ask for help. Use trivets or hot pads to protect counters.
• Draining hot foods can be tricky, too. The food will try to slide out with the fat or grease and has to be held back. It helps to have a third hand to do part of the chore. If you have permission to do it alone, have a metal can or plastic container (never glass) ready to receive the fat.
• Pots with handles hanging over the edge of the stove are bad news. Keep the handles turned away, where little people can't grab them and big people won't bump into them.

Unmolding Masterpieces
• To unmold a gelatin salad or dessert, run a thin knife between the gelatin and mold and turn it out on a chilled plate following either of these two methods:
• Dip the mold into hot water as deeply as you can without getting the salad wet. Hold it there for the count of 5 and remove. You want to loosen the gelatin, not melt it. Cover the mold with the plate and, holding the two together, turn upside down. Lift off the mold. Repeat the process if necessary.
• The second method is not as tricky but it takes more time. Turn the mold upside down on the plate. Dip a dish towel in hot water and wring out well. Place over the mold, pressing it into the design. Lift the mold, gently shaking it. Repeat until you hear the "plop" that means the salad is unmolded.

Clean-up Know-how
• Good cooks clean up as they go. Stack utensils and bowls in the sink as you are finished using them. Wash them before you begin the next recipe.
• Any spills should be wiped up pronto, especially those that land on the floor. Keep a roll of paper towels handy for this chore.
• Leave the kitchen as clean as you found it — that's part of the job.

SUMMER CELEBRATIONS

Step right up and be counted on the biggest bang-up birthday celebration of them all. Enjoy America's summertime holiday with these razzle-dazzle recipe ideas.

A flair for fireworks? Then cook up a cookout in your own backyard. Plan a carefree meal that tastes spectacular. It lets you prepare things ahead so you can have fun on the Fourth.

BEEF KEBABS
RISOTTO   THREE-BEAN SALAD
GRILLED HERBED BREAD
WATERMELON BOAT   FLAG CAKE
NATURAL TART LEMONADE

BEEF KEBABS

  1 cup lemon juice
  ½ cup salad oil or olive oil
  1 medium onion, grated
  2 cloves garlic, minced
1½ teaspoons paprika
1½ teaspoons pepper
  2 teaspoons salt
2½ pounds beef sirloin tip or top round, cut into 1-inch cubes
16 mushroom caps
  1 large onion, cut into 1-inch pieces
  2 green peppers, cut into 1-inch pieces

Combine lemon juice, oil, grated onion, garlic and seasonings. Pour over beef and marinate at least 2 hours in the refrigerator.

Drain beef cubes, reserving marinade. Thread meat on skewers alternately with mushroom caps, onion pieces and green peppers. Broil meat over hot coals (5 minutes for rare; 12 for well done), turning occasionally and basting with reserved marinade.

8 skewers.

RISOTTO

  1 medium onion, chopped
  ¼ cup butter or oil
  2 cups rice
  4 cups hot broth or bouillon (chicken or beef)
     Pinch of saffron (optional)
     Salt and pepper to taste
  ½ cup grated Parmesan cheese

In a saucepan, cook onion in butter until soft. Add rice and stir until all grains are well coated. Add hot broth and bring to a boil. (A pinch of saffron steeped in the broth 5 to 10 minutes will add a lovely color and aroma to the risotto.) Season with salt and pepper. Cover and reduce heat; simmer 15 to 20 minutes, until rice is tender. Top the cooked rice with grated cheese and toss lightly.

8 servings (¾ cup each).

THREE-BEAN SALAD

  1 can (16 ounces) red kidney beans
  1 can (16 ounces) white kidney beans
  1 can (16 ounces) cut green beans
  1 medium onion, sliced and separated into rings
  ¼ cup vinegar
  ½ cup salad oil
  ¼ teaspoon sugar
  ½ teaspoon salt
  ¼ teaspoon pepper
     Pinch each of thyme, basil and garlic powder

Drain beans and toss with onion rings. Combine remaining ingredients; pour over beans and toss well. Cover and chill several hours or overnight.

8 servings.

GRILLED HERBED BREAD

½ cup butter, softened
1 teaspoon dried parsley flakes
½ teaspoon thyme
½ teaspoon oregano or marjoram
½ teaspoon rosemary
1 loaf French bread

Cream butter with dried herbs. Cut French bread into diagonal slices, cutting down to but not through bottom crust. Spread butter mixture between slices.

Wrap loaf in foil and heat on side of grill over hot coals (or in 350° oven) 20 minutes or until heated through. Turn loaf 2 or 3 times during grilling. To serve, split open foil and break off slices.

WATERMELON BOAT

Cutting lengthwise, slice off the top third of a small whole watermelon. Remove fruit with a melon ball scoop or carve out the pulp and cut into neat cubes or wedges. Trim out any remaining fruit close to the rind and reserve. Using the rim of a small glass as a guide, trace a scalloped edge around the rim of the melon with the point of a sharp knife. Cut out scalloped edge and moisten with lemon juice.

Fill the bottom of the hollowed-out watermelon boat with reserved trimmings and some of the watermelon balls. Fill the remainder of the shell in three sections: red, white and blue. At one end, heap in the watermelon balls (or use a mixture of watermelon and other red fruits, such as strawberries). In the center, use honeydew melon balls, sliced bananas tossed in lemon juice, lemon sherbet or vanilla ice cream. (If sherbet or ice cream is used, be sure to assemble the boat just before serving and keep well chilled.) Fill the other end with blue fruits; blueberries are ideal, but blue or black grapes may also be used. Mound the fruits to give height.

FLAG CAKE

CAKE

1 cup butter
1½ cups granulated sugar
5 eggs, beaten
¼ cup milk
2 cups sifted flour
½ teaspoon salt

TOPPING

2 cups heavy cream
¼ cup confectioners' sugar
1 teaspoon cornstarch
½ teaspoon vanilla
2 pints uniformly sized strawberries
1 pint blueberries

Cream butter and granulated sugar until fluffy. Beat in eggs and milk. Gently fold in flour and salt. Turn batter into a greased and floured 13x9x2-inch cake pan. Bake in a preheated 350° oven 1 hour or until cake is firm in the center. Cool on a rack.

Whip cream until almost thick. Sift confectioners' sugar with cornstarch; add to cream with vanilla and beat until cream holds firm peaks.

Wash, hull and dry the strawberries. Wash and pick over blueberries. Spread the top and sides of the cake with ⅔ of the frosting. In the upper lefthand corner, mark off a rectangle (4 inches long by 3 inches deep) for the field of stars; arrange blueberries as "stars." Align rows of strawberries as stripes on the rest of the cake. Pipe the remaining frosting in bands between the strawberries. Refrigerate until ready to serve.

NATURAL TART LEMONADE

5 lemons, very thinly sliced
¾ cup sugar
2 quarts cold water

Place lemon slices in bottom of a wide bowl and sprinkle with sugar. Mash well with a wooden spoon and allow to stand 30 minutes. Add water and stir. Pour over ice cubes in tall glasses. Garnish with additional lemon slices.

8 tall glasses.

In the backyard, the park or at a tailgate party, here's a gourmet picnic that's great for summer.

GAZPACHO WITH GARNISHES
COLD DEVILED CHICKEN
PROVENÇALE RATATOUILLE LOAF
CHILLED MELON

GAZPACHO WITH GARNISHES

- 1 beef bouillon cube
- ¼ cup boiling water
- ¾ cup cold water
- 1 tablespoon lemon juice
- 1 tablespoon olive oil or salad oil
- 1 small red onion, cut up
- 1 small green pepper, seeded and cut up
- 1 small clove garlic, crushed
- ½ cucumber, peeled and cut up
- 2 tomatoes, peeled, cut and seeded
- 1 cup tomato juice
  Pinch each of salt and pepper
- 1 or 2 drops hot pepper sauce
  Garnishes (croutons, diced cucumber, chopped green pepper, chopped hard-boiled eggs)

Dissolve bouillon cube in boiling water. Pour into blender container and add all ingredients except tomatoes, tomato juice, seasonings and garnishes. Blend until very smooth. Add tomatoes and blend just until finely chopped. Stir in tomato juice and seasonings. Chill thoroughly. Carry to the picnic site in a chilled vacuum bottle. Pack garnishes in individual containers.

4 servings.

COLD DEVILED CHICKEN

- ½ cup vegetable oil
- 1 teaspoon chili powder
- 1 teaspoon salt
- 1 teaspoon paprika
- 1 teaspoon prepared mustard
- 1 broiler-fryer chicken (about 3 pounds), quartered

Combine oil and seasonings and mix well. Brush chicken pieces with the seasoned oil. Place chicken skin-side down on a rack in a foil-lined broiler pan. Broil 6 to 8 inches from heat, turning occasionally and brushing with oil, 30 minutes or until done.

Cool, wrap in foil and refrigerate until ready for the picnic basket.

4 servings.

PROVENÇALE RATATOUILLE LOAF

- ¼ cup olive oil
- 1 or 2 cloves garlic, minced
- 1 medium onion, diced
- 1 small eggplant, cut into 1-inch cubes
- 1 green pepper, seeded and diced
- 2 zucchini (about ½ pound), thinly sliced
- 1 can (16 ounces) tomatoes, drained
- 1 bay leaf
- ¼ teaspoon thyme
- ¼ teaspoon basil
  Salt and pepper to taste
- ¼ cup sliced black olives
- 1 loaf French bread

Heat olive oil in a large saucepan. Add garlic and onion and cook until onion is wilted. Add eggplant, green pepper and zucchini. Cook 5 minutes, stirring occasionally.

Break up tomatoes with a spoon and add to the eggplant mixture with the seasonings. Cover and cook over low heat about 30 minutes, stirring occasionally. For the last few minutes, uncover and boil down quickly to reduce juices — the mixture should be very thick. Remove bay leaf. Stir in olives; cool.

Cut a thick horizontal slice all along the loaf of bread, leaving one side attached. Open loaf and scoop out the soft insides from the base, leaving a fairly thick shell. Fill loaf with the vegetable mixture and replace the top slice, pressing lightly. Wrap in foil and refrigerate several hours or overnight. To serve, cut crosswise into thick slices.

4 servings.

NOTE: Don't let the scooped-out bread go to waste. Whirl in the blender for fresh crumbs. Or heat in the oven to dry and then whirl for dry crumbs.

TRICK OR TREAT

Let your imagination run free and put a fun face on Halloween. It's no trick to stir up these taste-tempting treats that are sure to please your youngsters.

Give a hearty Halloween send-off to a band of merry masqueraders. Select orange partyware and create a pumpkin patch with a special jack-o'-lantern cake. Encourage the guests to decorate the burgers with their own cheese cut-outs. They won't be able to mask their delight.

JACK-O'-LANTERN BURGERS
CARROT STICKS   CELERY STICKS
RIPE OLIVES
PUMPKIN CENTERPIECE CAKE
APPLE CIDER OR MILK

JACK-O'-LANTERN BURGERS

  2 pounds ground beef
1½ teaspoons salt
  1 teaspoon pepper
  ¼ cup tomato juice
  8 slices American cheese

Break up beef with a fork. Handling meat lightly, mix in salt, pepper and tomato juice. Gently form into 8 patties. Cook on a lightly greased hot skillet — for medium-rare, cook 5 minutes on one side until well browned, then turn and brown other side 3 minutes.

Meanwhile, cut jack-o'-lantern eyes, nose and mouth shapes out of each slice of cheese. Place a cut-out cheese slice on each patty and return to skillet to allow cheese to melt, cooking about 2 minutes longer. Serve open-face on hamburger buns or toasted English muffins.

8 servings.

NOTE: Allow for a little self-expression and have each youngster cut out the face for his or her burger.

PUMPKIN CENTERPIECE CAKE

  2 Halloween Pumpkin Cakes (page 37)
  ⅓ cup orange juice
  ½ cup granulated sugar
  1 package (3 ounces) cream cheese, softened
  3 cups confectioners' sugar
  ½ teaspoon vanilla
     Green food coloring

Make 2 Halloween Pumpkin Cakes, baking each in a Bundt pan. Cool completely. Cut a thin slice off the bottom of each cake to flatten the uneven surface caused by rising. Place the cakes, flattened surfaces together, on a serving dish, matching the ridges on the two cakes.

Cut out a curved horizontal wedge (about ½ inch deep) from one side of the bottom cake to make a jack-o'-lantern mouth. To form the nose, cut out a triangular wedge where the cakes join. Cut out 2 triangular wedges from the top cake to form the eyes.

Heat orange juice and granulated sugar until sugar is dissolved; cool. Prick cakes all over and drizzle evenly with orange syrup.

Beat cream cheese until smooth; gradually beat in confectioners' sugar, vanilla and food coloring. Beat until mixture holds together. Chill 10 minutes. Form some of mixture into leaves and place on top of cake. Spoon remainder onto waxed paper. Dust hands with confectioners' sugar and shape mixture to form a stem. Fit stem on top of cake, molding to shape as necessary.

HALLOWEEN SPECIALTIES

SPICED HOT APPLE CIDER

2 quarts apple cider or apple juice
1 cinnamon stick
6 whole cloves
1 teaspoon whole allspice
¼ cup brown sugar
8 orange slices (optional)

Combine all ingredients except orange slices in a saucepan and bring to a simmer. Simmer gently 5 to 10 minutes to extract all the flavor from the spices. Strain into mugs and garnish each with an orange slice.

8 servings (1 cup each).

GOBLIN COOKIES

1 cup butter
1 cup light brown sugar
1 egg
1 teaspoon vanilla
1¾ cups flour
1 teaspoon baking soda
1 teaspoon salt
1 tablespoon milk
3 cups quick-cooking oats (uncooked)
1 cup dark raisins

Cream butter until soft; gradually add brown sugar, beating until fluffy. Beat in egg and vanilla. Sift flour, baking soda and salt together; gradually stir into egg mixture. Stir in milk and oatmeal; mix well and chill for a few hours.

Roll out dough on a sheet of waxed paper until a little less than ¼ inch thick. With a jack-o'-lantern cutter, cut out cookies and place about 1 inch apart on a lightly greased baking sheet. Use raisins to make eyes, nose and mouth on each cookie. Bake in a preheated 375° oven 10 minutes.

About 40 cookies.

NOTE: Not all of the cookies need be shaped as jack-o'-lanterns. Try a variety of cookie cutters to bring out all the goblins — cats, witches and ghosts.

ORANGE DOUGHNUT DROPS

2 eggs
½ cup granulated sugar
2 tablespoons butter, softened
2 cups flour
2 teaspoons baking powder
¼ teaspoon salt
½ cup orange juice
2 tablespoons finely grated orange peel
Oil for deep frying
Confectioners' sugar

Beat eggs; then beat in granulated sugar and butter. Sift flour, baking powder and salt together; stir into egg mixture alternately with orange juice and peel.

Heat oil to 375° in a large saucepan or deep skillet. Drop batter into oil by scant teaspoonfuls — do not overcrowd. (The batter will drop easily if you dip spoon into hot oil before dipping it into batter.) Fry until golden brown, then turn to brown evenly. Remove with a slotted spoon. Drain on paper towels and dust with confectioners' sugar.

3 dozen 1½-inch doughnut drops.

 ENTERTAINING IDEAS

To create a unique Halloween decoration, select an assortment of dimensional characters and party favors and make a mobile. At the end of the party, give each guest an item from the mobile.

For a creative ghost story, seat children in a circle and give each one 30 seconds to add to a progressive ghost story. After the story, pass a sack of goodies and let each storyteller choose a treat.

Black crepe streamers can be part of your party decorations as well as a game. Before the party, wind several streamers of the same length around the room. (You'll need one for each child.) Start the streamers at different points, but have them all lead to the center of the web. Give each child a streamer. A prize goes to the first one to unravel the web.

POPCORN BALLS

- 1 cup light corn syrup
- ½ cup sugar
- 1 package (3 ounces) fruit-flavored gelatin
- 1 cup coarsely chopped peanuts
- 3 quarts popped popcorn (about ¾ cup unpopped)

Combine corn syrup and sugar in a large heavy saucepan; bring to a boil, stirring. Remove from heat and add gelatin, stirring until dissolved. Stir in peanuts and popcorn and mix well. When cool enough to handle, shape into balls with lightly buttered hands. Wrap each ball in plastic wrap and tie with orange ribbon or yarn.

12 popcorn balls.

Spicy old-fashioned goodness. Serve it plain or try a little witchery and turn it into a jolly centerpiece (see page 35).

HALLOWEEN PUMPKIN CAKE

- ½ cup butter
- 1½ cups sugar
- 3 eggs
- 1 teaspoon vanilla
- 2 cups flour
- 1 teaspoon baking powder
- 1 teaspoon baking soda
- 1 teaspoon cinnamon
- ½ teaspoon ground ginger
- ¼ teaspoon ground cloves
- 1 cup canned pumpkin or fresh pumpkin puree
- ¼ cup milk
- 1 cup chopped walnuts
- ¾ cup raisins

Cream butter and sugar until fluffy. Beat in eggs and vanilla. Sift flour with baking powder, baking soda and spices; stir into butter mixture alternately with pumpkin, ending with flour. Stir in milk, walnuts and raisins.

Pour batter into a greased and floured 10-inch Bundt pan. Bake in a preheated 350° oven 1 hour and 15 minutes or until cake tests done (stick a toothpick into the middle of the cake; if it comes out clean, the cake is done). Cool in pan 30 minutes, then turn out onto a cake rack to finish cooling.

CANDIED APPLES

- 6 medium apples
- 6 wooden skewers or sticks
- 2 cups sugar
- ⅔ cup light corn syrup
- 1 cup water
- Red food coloring

Wash and dry apples. Remove stem from each and insert a wooden skewer securely in its place.

In a small heavy saucepan, dissolve sugar and corn syrup in water over medium heat. Raise heat and boil rapidly until syrup reaches 300° on a candy thermometer — the hard crack stage. (No thermometer? Drop a little of the mixture into very cold water; when removed, it will crack when tapped sharply.) Remove from heat and stir in enough food coloring to give a bright rosy color.

Place saucepan in a large pan of hot water. Holding each apple by its skewer, dip into syrup until completely coated; place on a greased tray or cookie sheet to harden.

6 candied apples.

LET US GIVE THANKS

Celebrate Thanksgiving with a bountiful feast for the entire family. On this uniquely American holiday, fill your table with an array of traditional fall favorites.

Whether you're planning a small gathering or calling together the entire family for a reunion, Thanksgiving is the time for a feast. Plan your dinner around the customary Thanksgiving turkey and fill the table with a bountiful selection of harvest foods. This menu is ideal for 8 to 10, but can be increased easily to accommodate 20 (see page 42 for instructions).

OYSTERS IN WRAPS
CREAM OF FRESH MUSHROOM SOUP
TURKEY WITH TWO STUFFINGS
TURKEY GRAVY
YAM PUFF
BRUSSELS SPROUTS WITH CHESTNUTS
CRANBERRY-ORANGE-PEAR RELISH
APPLE TART   PERFECT PUMPKIN PIE

OYSTERS IN WRAPS

10 slices bacon
20 small shucked oysters

Cut each bacon slice in half. Wrap each oyster in a piece of bacon and secure with a wooden pick. Arrange on a rack on a broiler pan and broil about 4 inches from heat. Turn after 3 minutes to brown bacon on all sides. Serve as hors d'oeuvres.

10 servings (2 oysters each).

NOTE: No oysters? Substitute 20 pitted dried prunes for the oysters. If you like, stuff prunes with small square of Cheddar cheese or a dab of peanut butter before wrapping in bacon. Broil as directed above.

CREAM OF FRESH MUSHROOM SOUP

1 pound fresh mushrooms
¼ cup butter
¼ cup flour
1½ quarts chicken broth
2 cups light cream
¼ teaspoon thyme
   Pinch of cayenne pepper
   Salt to taste

Wipe mushrooms clean with a moist paper towel; trim off the stem ends. Melt butter in a large saucepan; gradually add flour, stirring to make a paste. Add 1 cup of the broth and stir until slightly thickened. Add remaining broth and bring to a boil, stirring occasionally. Reduce heat and simmer 4 to 5 minutes.

Cut up mushrooms and puree in a blender or food processor with a small amount of the broth. Add the mushroom puree to the broth; then stir in cream. Season with thyme, cayenne pepper and salt and simmer 4 to 5 minutes longer — do not boil.

8 to 10 servings (about ¾ cup each).

NOTE: If you plan to hold the soup before serving, or if you choose to prepare it ahead of time, place in a large pan of hot water to keep warm or to reheat. Do not place over direct heat. Add cream just before reheating.

TURKEY WITH TWO STUFFINGS

1 turkey (12 pounds)
1 tablespoon salt
2 teaspoons pepper
½ cup dry white wine or white vermouth
Fruit and Sausage Stuffing (below)
Wild Rice Stuffing (right)
¼ cup butter, melted

Remove giblets from turkey. Rub turkey inside and out with salt and pepper and sprinkle cavity with about 3 tablespoons of the wine.

Fill body cavity loosely with Fruit and Sausage Stuffing; do not pack tightly. Fill neck cavity with Wild Rice Stuffing. Sew or skewer openings and truss legs and wings against body. Place turkey on a rack in a roasting pan and brush with melted butter. Roast in a preheated 325° oven about 4 hours, basting occasionally with pan drippings and with remaining wine. The turkey is done when leg joint moves easily and when a meat thermometer inserted in center of stuffing registers 165°. Remove from oven and let rest, tented with foil, in a warm place 15 minutes before carving.

8 to 10 servings.

FRUIT AND SAUSAGE STUFFING

1 pound sausage meat
½ cup butter
1 cup chopped onion
1 cup chopped celery
2 quarts bread cubes
2 cups cut-up mixed dried fruits
1 teaspoon marjoram
1 teaspoon salt
½ teaspoon pepper
½ teaspoon sage
½ cup water or turkey broth

Brown sausage meat in a large skillet, stirring with a fork. Remove meat to a large bowl, pouring off fat. Add butter, onion and celery to skillet and cook over medium heat, stirring, 5 minutes. Add bread cubes, turning to brown. Add mixture to sausage in bowl. Add remaining ingredients and toss until well mixed. Adjust seasoning to taste. Cool before using to stuff turkey.

Makes enough stuffing for a 12-pound turkey.

WILD RICE STUFFING

1 package (6 ounces) long grain and wild rice blend
½ cup chopped onion
⅓ cup chopped walnuts
3 tablespoons butter

Prepare the rice blend in a saucepan as directed on label, but reduce water to 2 cups and cooking time to 20 minutes. Sauté onion and walnuts in butter until onion is soft; stir into rice mixture. Cool before using to stuff neck cavity.

TURKEY GRAVY

Neck and gizzard from turkey
4 cups water
1 stalk celery
1 small onion
1 bay leaf
Salt and pepper to taste
2 whole cloves
2 tablespoons flour
1 hard-boiled egg, chopped
Pinch of sage

While turkey is roasting, make broth for gravy: Place turkey neck and gizzard in a saucepan with water, celery, onion, bay leaf, salt, pepper and cloves. Bring to a boil and skim off foam. Cover and simmer about 1¼ hours or until gizzard is tender. Cool. Strain broth, reserving gizzard. Chop gizzard meat very finely, discarding fat and sinews.

After turkey has been removed from roasting pan, skim off excess fat from drippings remaining in pan. Sprinkle flour into pan, stirring to incorporate all the brown bits on the side. Cook over low heat until thickened, stirring constantly. Gradually add 1½ cups strained turkey broth, the chopped gizzard, hard-boiled egg, sage and more salt and pepper to taste. Bring to a boil, stirring until well blended. Pour into a gravy boat.

About 1½ cups.

YAM PUFF

    4 cups cut-up cooked or canned yams
         or sweet potatoes
    ¼ cup butter, melted
    ½ cup light cream
    4 eggs, separated
    ¾ teaspoon salt
    ¼ teaspoon pepper
    ⅛ teaspoon cinnamon
    4 egg whites

Mash yams with melted butter in a large bowl. Beat in cream, egg yolks, salt, pepper and cinnamon. Beat egg whites (8) until stiff but not dry and fold into yam mixture. Spoon into a buttered 6-cup soufflé dish. Bake in a preheated 325° oven 30 minutes or until puffed and golden.

8 to 10 servings.

NOTE: To cook yams or sweet potatoes, cover and boil in just enough salted water to cover until they can be pierced easily with a fork, about 40 minutes. Drain and rinse in cold water. Peel when cool enough to handle.

BRUSSELS SPROUTS WITH CHESTNUTS

    1 can (20 ounces) whole chestnuts
    2 pints fresh Brussels sprouts
    3 tablespoons butter
    ⅛ teaspoon ground nutmeg
       Salt and pepper to taste

Drain chestnuts, reserving ¼ cup of the liquid. Trim off stems of sprouts, cutting an **X** in the base of each one to ensure even cooking. Rinse sprouts and cook, uncovered, in a small amount of boiling salted water 10 to 12 minutes or until crisp-tender. Drain.

In a large heavy saucepan, heat butter, reserved chestnut liquid and chestnuts until slightly glazed. Add sprouts and seasonings, stirring until glazed.

8 to 10 servings.

NOTE: When shopping for fresh Brussels sprouts, look for a bright green color and leaves that are compact and unblemished.

CRANBERRY-ORANGE-PEAR RELISH

    2 small oranges (peeled or unpeeled)
    1 firm pear
    1 pound fresh cranberries
  1¼ cups sugar

Quarter oranges and discard center pith and seeds. Quarter pear and discard core and seeds. Pick over cranberries and rinse. Put oranges, pear and cranberries through a food chopper. Add sugar and mix well. Chill at least 1 hour.

3 to 4 cups.

APPLE TART

       9-inch Cookie Crust Pie Shell (page 42)
    ½ cup cookie crumbs (any kind but chocolate)
    3 pounds tart cooking apples
    ½ cup sugar
    ½ teaspoon cinnamon
    3 tablespoons lemon juice
    ½ cup raspberry or strawberry jelly

Prepare Cookie Crust Pie Shell; chill.

Spread cookie crumbs evenly over bottom of pie shell. Peel and core apples; slice into thin wedges and toss lightly with sugar, cinnamon and lemon juice. Transfer apples to chilled unbaked pie shell, arranging the top layer in concentric circles. Bake in a preheated 350° oven 50 minutes or until crust is golden and apples are tender.

Warm jelly to soften and pour evenly over apples. Bake pie 5 minutes longer to glaze. Serve warm or cool. If desired, top each serving with a dollop of whipped cream.

NOTE: For an open-faced tart, it's best to use apples with a firm texture so that the slices will retain their shape after baking. Excellent choices are Jersey Red and Rome Beauty; also good are Golden Delicious, Granny Smith, Rhode Island Greening and Newtown Pippin.

PERFECT PUMPKIN PIE

9-inch Cookie Crust Pie Shell (below)
1 cup sugar
1 tablespoon flour
½ teaspoon salt
1 teaspoon ground ginger
¾ teaspoon cinnamon
⅛ teaspoon ground nutmeg
2½ cups canned pumpkin or fresh pumpkin puree
2 tablespoons molasses
2 tablespoons butter, melted
3 eggs
1½ cups milk

Prepare Cookie Crust Pie Shell; chill.

Combine sugar, flour, salt, ginger, cinnamon and nutmeg in a large mixing bowl. Add pumpkin, molasses and melted butter; whisk or stir well to combine. Beat eggs slightly, then stir in milk; blend into pumpkin mixture. Pour filling into chilled unbaked pie shell and bake in a preheated 425° oven about 40 minutes or until golden brown and set.

COOKIE CRUST PIE SHELL

1¼ cups sifted flour
¼ teaspoon salt
2 tablespoons sugar
½ cup butter, softened
1 egg yolk
1 tablespoon lemon juice

Spoon flour and salt into a large bowl. Push to sides of bowl, leaving a space in center. Drop sugar, butter, egg yolk and lemon juice into center space. Cream center ingredients, gradually working in the flour. Gather dough into a ball, then knead a few times on a flat surface. Wrap in waxed paper and chill until ready to use (at least 1 hour).

On a lightly floured surface, roll dough out until slightly larger than pie plate. Fit loosely into the plate, then turn edge under all around; flute. Place shell in freezer or refrigerator to chill while preparing filling. (The pie shell may be prepared ahead and frozen.)

Makes one 8- or 9-inch pie shell.

🦃 DINNER FOR 20

For some, Thanksgiving means a crowd. This menu can still fill the bill. Here's how to adapt it:

To Start
• Make Oysters in Wraps using 15 slices bacon and 30 small oysters — not everyone will want extras.
• In addition, serve Chopped Chicken Liver (page 43), made with turkey liver as well as chicken liver.

Soup
• Double the recipe for the soup.

Turkey and Stuffings
• Use a 20- to 22-pound turkey (or prepare two 12-pounders for more drumsticks and wings).
• Double all the ingredients for Fruit and Sausage Stuffing *except* the sausage meat and dried fruit — there will be enough to flavor the bird.
• To extend the Wild Rice Stuffing for the neck cavity, beat 2 eggs and stir into the rice mixture.

Gravy
• When making the broth, use 1½ quarts water and increase the seasonings. Sprinkle ¼ cup flour into the pan and add 3 cups strained turkey broth.

Vegetables
• Don't make the Yam Puff for a large party. Instead prepare Candied Yams: Arrange cooked or canned yam halves (about 20) in a buttered baking dish. Drizzle with honey or brown sugar, dot with butter and ladle about 1 cup turkey broth over to moisten. Bake in a preheated 325° oven about 30 minutes.
• For the Brussels Sprouts with Chestnuts, use 4 pints of sprouts; increase seasonings to taste.
• If you like, add Creamed Onions (page 48).

Relishes
• Double the recipe for the relish.

Dessert
• Add Cold Eggnog Soufflé (page 69) to the pies.

Leftovers
• Now it's time to relax — you deserve it. Slice the leftover turkey and have it ready and waiting for sandwiches. (If you like, heat the slices in gravy and serve open-face.) Cut down on clean-up time by serving on Hallmark Thanksgiving paper partyware.

HAPPY HANUKKAH

Add extra meaning to this happy mid-winter festival with the personal touch only you can give. Surprise your family with a delicious new approach to a tradition.

Hanukkah is a time of togetherness. And what better way to celebrate than with a special family dinner, based on tradition but touched with imagination. The following menu is well suited to this busy time of year since virtually everything, except the latkes, can be prepared well in advance. (Remember, too, creatively wrapped in a box or gift tin, Rugelach makes a thoughtful Hanukkah gift.)

CHOPPED CHICKEN LIVER
PARTY POT ROAST
POTATO LATKES   PINK APPLESAUCE
RUGELACH

CHOPPED CHICKEN LIVER

½ pound chicken livers
1 onion, sliced
6 tablespoons chicken fat or margarine
2 hard-boiled eggs
   Salt and pepper to taste

Remove any fat from the livers. Sauté livers and onion slices in 4 tablespoons chicken fat until liver is almost cooked through but still pink in the center. Transfer to a chopping bowl or food processor. Add eggs, seasonings and remaining chicken fat. Chop or swirl together to make a paste. Serve with crackers or slices of egg bread.

About 2 cups.

NOTE: Mounded high and sprinkled with chopped parsley, Chopped Chicken Liver makes a marvelous party spread. You can prepare it 2 to 3 days in advance if you keep it tightly covered and refrigerated. It can also be used as an alternative to liver pâté in a *Beef Wellington* (see page 74).

PARTY POT ROAST

   3-pound pot roast (brisket or chuck)
¼ cup flour
1 tablespoon salt
⅛ teaspoon pepper
1 teaspoon paprika
2 tablespoons fat or margarine
8 small white onions
1 can (8 ounces) tomato sauce
½ cup beef broth or red wine
2 tablespoons brown sugar
4 to 8 carrots, cut into chunks

Dust pot roast with mixture of flour, salt, pepper and paprika. Heat fat in a heavy pot and brown meat on all sides. Add onions, turning to glaze. Add tomato sauce and broth; cover and simmer 2 hours. Add sugar and carrots and simmer, covered, 30 minutes longer or until meat is tender. Serve immediately or cool in sauce, then reheat. (The meat slices more easily when cold, and the flavor improves with reheating in the pan sauce.)

Enough for 2 meals (3 to 4 servings each).

NOTE: Plan ahead for a second meal. Slice the remaining meat and arrange with the vegetables in a freeze-heat-and-serve dish. Skim excess fat from the sauce and pour over meat and vegetables. (You can use the skimmed-off fat to season other dishes.) Cover and refrigerate or freeze; reheat in a 325° oven. If desired, top with mashed potatoes.

POTATO LATKES

2 large baking potatoes or 4 medium potatoes, peeled
1 small onion
2 eggs
2 tablespoons flour
1 teaspoon salt
¼ teaspoon white pepper
Vegetable oil

Finely grate potatoes into a large bowl. Grate onion into bowl. Drain off excess potato liquid. Beat in eggs, then stir in flour, salt and pepper.

Heat about ¼ inch oil in a large skillet. Drop potato mixture by tablespoonfuls into hot oil. Brown just until edges are crisp; turn and brown other sides. Remove with a slotted spoon and serve hot. Latkes are traditionally served with applesauce.

4 servings.

PINK APPLESAUCE

2 pounds McIntosh or Cortland apples
2 tablespoons lemon juice
2 tablespoons sugar

Remove stem and blossom ends from apples. Cut into wedges, peels and pits included, and drop into cooking pan. Add about 1 inch of water. Cover and cook until apples are soft, about 10 minutes. Force through a food mill or strainer to eliminate skin and seeds. Season with lemon juice and sugar, adjusting to taste. Stir. Serve warm or chilled.

About 2 cups.

NOTE: Don't worry about adding too little water to the apples in the pan. Worry about too much; it dilutes the sauce. You need only enough water to keep the apples from burning. Taste the sauce before adding the sugar. In applesauce, it serves as a seasoner rather than a sweetener.

RUGELACH

2 cups flour
½ teaspoon salt
⅔ cup shortening
1 tablespoon sugar
1 egg yolk
1 tablespoon grated orange peel
¼ cup orange juice
⅔ cup sugar
2 tablespoons cinnamon
¼ cup margarine, melted
½ cup currants or raisins
½ cup chopped walnuts
1 egg yolk
1 tablespoon water

Combine flour and salt in a bowl. Cut in shortening with a pastry blender or 2 knives until mixture resembles coarse meal. Blend in 1 tablespoon sugar and 1 egg yolk. Add orange peel and juice and mix in gently. Knead the dough a few times to form a smooth ball. Divide in half and wrap each half in waxed paper; chill at least 1 hour.

Mix ⅔ cup sugar and the cinnamon. Have the margarine, currants and walnuts ready to work with, but do not combine.

Working with one ball of dough at a time, roll out to a 12-inch circle on a floured board with a lightly floured rolling pin. Brush the circle with half the melted margarine. Sprinkle with half the sugar-cinnamon mixture, then with half the currants and half the nuts. Press the currants and nuts very lightly into the dough with your hand or the rolling pin.

Using a long, sharp knife, cut the pastry circle into 12 pie-shaped wedges. Starting at the wide outer end, carefully roll up each wedge toward its point, handling gently to avoid tearing the dough. Place point down and about 1 inch apart on a lightly greased baking sheet. Twist end of each roll slightly inward to form a crescent. Dust any bits of nuts and sugar from pastry surface. Repeat with the remaining dough and filling.

Beat the remaining egg yolk and water; brush on the tops of the pastries. Bake in a preheated 350° oven about 30 minutes or until golden brown.

2 dozen pastries.

SEASON'S GREETINGS

Spread holiday cheer throughout the yuletide season with distinctive dinners, festive desserts and old-fashioned goodies. They're gifts from the kitchen and you.

Present your own happy version of a Christmas past with this dinner reminiscent of Dickens' classic.

ROAST GOOSE WITH STUFFING AND GRAVY
HERBED CARROTS AND GREEN BEANS
CREAMED ONIONS
PLUM PUDDING WITH BRANDIED HARD SAUCE

ROAST GOOSE WITH STUFFING AND GRAVY

- 1 goose (about 10 pounds)
- 2 tablespoons salt
- 1 teaspoon pepper
- 2 teaspoons caraway seeds

STUFFING
- 4 medium apples, cored and diced
- 1 pound pitted dried prunes
- 1 cup water
- 1 medium onion, diced
- 1 tablespoon butter or vegetable oil
- 1½ cups bread crumbs
  Salt, pepper and cayenne pepper to taste
- ½ cup white wine (optional)

GRAVY
- Goose neck, gizzard, heart, wing tips
- 1 small onion, sliced
- 3 cups water
- 2 tablespoons cornstarch
- ¼ cup port wine or cold water
  Salt, pepper and cayenne pepper to taste

Rinse goose. Cut off wing tips and reserve. Pull excess lumps of fat from body cavity and wipe goose inside and out with paper towels. Rub inside and out with mixture of salt, pepper and caraway seeds.

To make stuffing, combine apples, prunes and water in a saucepan; cover and simmer until fruits are soft. Cook onion in butter (or render some of the fat trimmed from goose for cooking the onion) until it begins to soften. Add onion, bread crumbs and seasonings to fruit and mix well. If stuffing is too dry, add wine or a little water. Cool thoroughly before stuffing goose.

Fill body cavity lightly with stuffing; do not pack tightly, as stuffing will expand during cooking. Sew or skewer opening and truss legs and wings tightly against body. Place goose, breast up, on a rack in a shallow roasting pan. Roast in a preheated 350° oven about 2½ hours, draining off fat as it accumulates. Baste goose occasionally with the pan juices. The goose is done when leg joint moves easily and juices run pale yellow (rather than pink) when the fleshy part of the thigh is pricked with a skewer.

Place goose on serving platter and remove skewers and trussing strings. Let stand in a warm place for 10 to 15 minutes before carving; remove stuffing to a serving bowl.

Meanwhile, make gravy. First brown neck, gizzard, heart, wing tips and sliced onion under a broiler. Add to water in a large saucepan and let simmer while the goose is roasting, about 2 hours. Strain. Liquid should have reduced to about 2 cups; if not, reduce further or add water as necessary. When goose is done, pour off excess fat from roasting pan; add goose stock and cook 1 to 2 minutes, stirring in all the brown bits that cling to the bottom and sides of the pan. Dissolve cornstarch in port; add to the pan and cook, stirring, until thick and clear. Add seasonings. Strain and serve in a gravy boat.

6 servings (with leftovers).

46

HERBED CARROTS AND GREEN BEANS

1 pound fresh green beans
¾ pound fresh carrots
1½ tablespoons butter
¾ cup water
¼ teaspoon salt
2 tablespoons chopped fresh parsley or
   2 teaspoons mixed dried herbs (parsley, chervil, marjoram)

Trim beans and cut into 2-inch sections; cook, uncovered, in boiling salted water until just tender, about 10 to 15 minutes. Drain.

Scrape carrots and cut into 2-inch strips, about the size of the beans. Heat butter in a heavy saucepan and add carrots, tossing to coat. Add water and salt; cover and simmer 30 minutes or until carrots are tender and most of liquid has evaporated. Uncover and add drained beans; toss until beans are hot and coated with butter. Sprinkle with herbs and toss gently.

4 to 6 servings.

CREAMED ONIONS

1 pound small white onions, peeled
4 whole cloves
1½ tablespoons butter
1½ tablespoons flour
¾ cup milk
2 tablespoons light or heavy cream
   Salt, pepper and ground nutmeg to taste

Cook onions and cloves, covered, in boiling salted water until tender, about 25 minutes. Drain and discard cloves.

Melt butter in a saucepan and stir in flour. Cook over low heat 1 to 2 minutes, stirring — do not let mixture brown. Slowly add milk, stirring over medium heat until thickened and smooth. Stir in cream and season with salt, pepper and nutmeg. Add onions and heat through.

4 to 6 servings.

PLUM PUDDING

¼ cup shortening
3 tablespoons brown sugar
1 egg
¾ cup flour
1 teaspoon baking powder
½ teaspoon baking soda
½ teaspoon cinnamon
¼ teaspoon ground allspice
¼ teaspoon ground nutmeg
1 teaspoon grated orange peel
½ cup raisins
½ cup dried figs or prunes, diced
¼ cup chopped walnuts
½ cup soft bread crumbs
½ cup quick-cooking oats (uncooked)
1½ cups applesauce
¼ cup molasses
¼ cup rum
   Brandied Hard Sauce (below)

Cream shortening and sugar until light; beat in egg. Toss together flour, baking powder, baking soda, spices, orange peel, fruits, nuts, bread crumbs and oats. Mix applesauce with molasses and rum and add to the creamed mixture alternately with the flour mixture, mixing well after each addition.

Pour into a greased 1-quart heatproof bowl or pudding basin; cover with greased foil or a double-thickness of greased waxed paper and tie with string. Stand bowl on a rack in a large kettle; add enough boiling water to come halfway up the side of the bowl and steam over low heat 2 to 2½ hours or until firm. Remove from heat and cool slightly. Unmold and serve warm with Brandied Hard Sauce. (If pudding is made ahead, resteam 30 minutes.)

6 servings.

NOTE: To flame pudding, warm (do not boil) 2 tablespoons brandy in a small saucepan. Spoon the warm brandy over the warm pudding and ignite immediately.

BRANDIED HARD SAUCE

½ cup butter, softened
1 cup sifted confectioners' sugar
1 tablespoon brandy

Cream butter until fluffy. Gradually beat in sugar until smooth, then beat in brandy.

Bring joy to family and friends with a classic dinner of English roast beef and bûche de Noël from France.

OYSTER SOUP
ROAST RIBS OF BEEF AU JUS
YORKSHIRE PUDDING
HORSERADISH SAUCE
GREEN BEAN CASSEROLE
BUCHE DE NOEL

OYSTER SOUP

    3 tablespoons butter
    ½ cup finely chopped celery
    ¼ cup finely chopped onion
    ¼ cup finely chopped carrot
    3 tablespoons flour
    1 pint shucked oysters, with their liquor
    3 cups milk
    1 teaspoon salt
    ¼ teaspoon pepper
    1 cup light or heavy cream, warmed
    2 tablespoons chopped fresh parsley (optional)
       Oyster crackers

Heat butter in a saucepan; add celery, onion and carrot and cook over medium heat 3 minutes, stirring occasionally. Sprinkle in flour and stir to blend in; cook 2 minutes longer. Drain oysters and add their liquor to the vegetables, stirring well. Stir in milk and add seasonings. Simmer gently 10 to 15 minutes or until vegetables are tender.

Add drained oysters and return to simmering point — do not boil. Cook only until edges of oysters curl, 1 to 2 minutes. Stir in cream. Pour into a tureen and sprinkle with parsley. Serve with oyster crackers.

6 to 8 servings.

ROAST RIBS OF BEEF AU JUS

       2-rib beef roast (about 5 pounds)
       Salt and pepper
    2 cups hot water or beef broth

Rub roast with salt and pepper. Insert meat thermometer in thickest part of meat, away from fat and bone. Place meat, fat side up, in a roasting pan — the bones will serve as a natural rack. Roast in a preheated 325° oven about 18 minutes per pound for rare (140° on the thermometer), 22 minutes per pound for medium (160° on the thermometer). When ready to make pudding, skim fat from pan.

Remove roast from pan when done to desired degree and let stand in a warm place 20 minutes before carving. Skim any fat from pan. Pour hot water into pan and bring to a simmer, stirring to scrape up all the brown bits on bottom and side of pan. Season with salt and pepper. Pour into gravy boat and serve as sauce with the meat.

6 to 8 servings.

NOTE: If you have a double oven, use one for the Yorkshire Pudding and the other for the Roast Beef and the Green Bean Casserole, putting the casserole in to bake while the roast rests. If you have but one oven, remove the roast about 20 minutes before it should be done and prepare Yorkshire Pudding. Put both the pudding and the roast in at 425° for 15 minutes; then remove roast and let it stand. Reduce oven temperature for pudding and add the Green Bean Casserole to oven; they bake together for 20 minutes.

YORKSHIRE PUDDING

    1½ cups flour
     ½ teaspoon salt
      3 eggs
      2 cups milk
     ¼ cup fat from roast beef

Put flour and salt in a bowl; make a well in center and break in eggs. Stir in 1 cup of the milk, blending smoothly. Beat with a wooden spoon or whisk 5 minutes. Stir in remaining milk. Allow to stand at least 1 hour at room temperature.

Measure fat into a 13x9x2-inch baking pan. Place pan in a preheated 425° oven for 2 minutes to heat fat. Remove from oven and pour in batter. Bake at 425° for 15 minutes; reduce heat to 350° and continue baking 20 minutes longer or until well risen on sides and golden in center.

6 to 8 servings.

HORSERADISH SAUCE

3 tablespoons butter
3 tablespoons flour
¾ cup beef broth
¾ cup milk
 Salt and white pepper to taste
3 tablespoons prepared horseradish
1 teaspoon dry mustard
2 tablespoons heavy cream

Melt butter in a small heavy saucepan; blend in flour with a whisk. Heat broth and milk; add to butter-flour mixture, stirring vigorously with whisk over medium heat until smooth and thick. Season with salt and pepper and simmer gently 10 minutes to remove any raw flour taste. Add horseradish, mustard and cream; stir and serve.

About 1½ cups.

GREEN BEAN CASSEROLE

1½ pounds fresh green beans, trimmed, or
  2 packages (10 ounces each) frozen beans
4 slices bacon
1 medium onion, chopped
4 large fresh tomatoes, peeled and chopped,
  or 1 can (16 ounces) tomatoes, drained and
  chopped
¼ teaspoon salt
 Pinch of pepper
¼ cup grated Swiss cheese
¼ cup grated Parmesan cheese

Cook beans in boiling salted water about 10 minutes, until tender but still crisp; drain. (Or cook frozen beans according to package directions.)

Cook bacon in a skillet until crisp. Drain on paper towels and crumble. Drain all but 1 tablespoon bacon fat from the skillet; add onion and cook, stirring occasionally, until tender.

Combine beans, bacon, onion, tomatoes, salt and pepper in a baking dish. Mix cheeses and sprinkle on top. Bake in a preheated 350° oven until cheese is golden brown, 15 to 20 minutes.

6 to 8 servings.

If you prefer rolls instead of, or in addition to, the Yorkshire Pudding, choose your favorite.

HOME-STYLE DINNER ROLLS

1 package active dry yeast
3 tablespoons sugar
1 cup warm water (about 110°)
1 cup milk
2 teaspoons salt
¼ cup vegetable oil or melted butter
6 to 6½ cups flour

Dissolve yeast and sugar in warm water in a large bowl; let stand 5 minutes. Warm milk until just tepid and add to yeast mixture along with salt and oil. Stir in 3 cups of the flour and beat until smooth. Add another 3 cups flour to make a soft dough. Knead on a floured board until smooth and elastic, adding additional flour as necessary to keep dough from sticking.

Place dough in a large oiled bowl; turn dough to coat lightly with the oil. Cover and let rise in a warm place until double in bulk, about 1½ hours. Punch down dough and knead again; let rise until double, about 1 hour.

Punch down dough and shape into your choice of dinner rolls listed below. Let rise until almost double, about 45 minutes. Bake in a preheated 400° oven until nicely browned, 15 to 20 minutes.

25 to 30 rolls.

PARKER HOUSE ROLLS

Roll dough ¼ inch thick and cut circles with a biscuit cutter. Brush with melted butter. Make a crease across center of each; fold in half along the crease. Place rolls close together in a greased baking pan.

CLOVERLEAF ROLLS

Form dough into 1-inch balls. Place 3 balls in each greased muffin cup.

CRESCENT ROLLS

Roll dough ⅛ inch thick and cut into strips 5 inches wide. Cut each strip into triangles, 4 inches wide at base. Holding the two lower points, stretch the base of the triangle slightly and then roll up, beginning at base. Place on a greased baking sheet with tip underneath and bend into a crescent shape.

BUCHE DE NOEL

- **4 eggs**
- **¾ cup granulated sugar**
- **1 teaspoon vanilla**
- **¾ cup flour**
- **1 teaspoon salt**
- **Confectioners' sugar**
- **Mocha Butter Cream (below)**
- **Marzipan Snowmen and Holly Leaves (right)**
- **Meringue Mushrooms (right)**

Line a 15x10-inch jelly roll pan with waxed paper. Grease the paper. Break eggs into the top of a double boiler over hot water. Add sugar and beat with whisk or hand beater until thick and creamy. Remove from heat. Add vanilla and beat until cool. Sift flour and salt over the mixture and fold in gently.

Pour batter evenly into the jelly roll pan. Bake in a preheated 400° oven 12 to 15 minutes or until cake is golden and springs back when touched in center. Turn cake out onto a kitchen towel dusted with confectioners' sugar; carefully remove waxed paper. Trim off all cake edges. Place a sheet of waxed paper on warm cake and roll up the cake with the paper inside. When cool, carefully unroll cake and remove paper. Spread a thin layer of Mocha Butter Cream on cake and roll up again.

Cut a diagonal slice from each end of the roll. Set the slices at an angle on the "log" to form branch stubs. Frost completely with Mocha Butter Cream. Use a fork to make "bark" lines. Chill just to set. Before serving, decorate with Marzipan Snowmen, Holly Leaves and Meringue Mushrooms. If desired, dust *bûche* lightly with confectioners' sugar to resemble snow.

6 to 8 servings.

MOCHA BUTTER CREAM

- **⅔ cup sugar**
- **¼ cup water**
- **5 egg yolks**
- **1 cup butter, softened**
- **1 tablespoon instant coffee powder**
- **1 teaspoon hot water**
- **2 ounces semisweet chocolate, melted**

Dissolve sugar in water over moderate heat. Raise heat and boil until syrup reaches 238° on a candy thermometer — the soft ball stage. (No thermometer? Drop a little of the mixture into very cold water; when removed, it will form a soft ball.)

Beat egg yolks lightly. Pour in the hot sugar syrup in a thin stream, beating constantly. When all sugar has been added, continue to beat until the mixture is cool, about 5 minutes more. It should be light and thick.

Add softened butter a little at a time, beating in each addition thoroughly before adding more. Dissolve instant coffee in hot water; add to the butter cream along with the melted chocolate, beating just until incorporated.

2 cups.

MARZIPAN SNOWMEN AND HOLLY LEAVES

Use a small package of marzipan and knead until it is smooth and pliable. (Dust lightly with confectioners' sugar if it becomes too oily.) Pinch off small pieces and roll into balls to make heads and bodies of snowmen. Assemble by moistening surfaces with a little water to make them stick. Make facial features with the ends of cloves or with tiny flakes of chocolate. Place on *bûche*.

Tint remaining marzipan with a few drops of green food coloring; roll out ⅛ inch thick on a board dusted with confectioners' sugar. Cut out holly leaves with a cookie cutter or knife. Place on *bûche*.

MERINGUE MUSHROOMS

Combine 1 egg white and ¼ cup sugar in heavy bowl and set it over a pot of boiling water — do not let the bowl touch the water. Beat with a whisk or hand-held electric mixer until the mixture is lukewarm. Remove from heat and continue to beat to make a stiff meringue.

Spoon meringue into a pastry bag and, using a plain tip, pipe out small domes onto a greased and floured baking sheet. Make ½-inch domes for mushroom caps and small pointed ones for stems. Dust caps lightly with unsweetened cocoa powder. Bake in a preheated 225° oven about 40 minutes. Remove from oven and stick caps to stems, using a little leftover meringue to stick them together if necessary. Press clusters into the *bûche*.

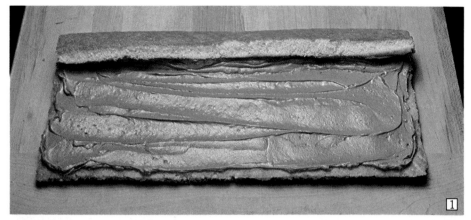

1. *Bûche de Noël starts with a simple sponge cake. While still warm, it is rolled up with a sheet of waxed paper (to prevent the cake from sticking to itself). Warm rolling keeps the cake flexible so that when cool, it can be unrolled, filled and then rerolled without tearing.*

2. *Be sure to cut off the ends of the roll at an angle. Place on opposite sides of the roll, as shown, to resemble the stubs of branches. Use dabs of frosting to hold them in place.*

3. *The finished Bûche de Noël represents a Yule log, complete with "bark" and woodland touches.*

CHRISTMAS GIFTS FROM YOUR KITCHEN

Cookies and candies, herbed vinegars and teas, fruitcakes and preserves — fill the house with the cheery aroma of gifts you make yourself. Whether you start your preparations well in advance or prefer the excitement of last-minute "doings," this recipe collection offers something for everyone.

Here's an ideal centerpiece for a party table — or use as a decoration almost anywhere in the house.

CHRISTMAS COOKIE CENTERPIECE

Follow the recipes for Chocolate Gingerbread Cookies (right) and Christmas Sugar Cookies (page 56) as directed except increase the flour by ½ cup in each recipe. (Since the cookies are going to be handled a good deal, a firmer dough is preferable — but the cookies will still be good to eat.) Be sure to cut a variety of shapes: bells, stars, Christmas stockings, Christmas trees, Santas. Before baking, make a small hole at the top of each cookie. Bake cookies as directed in the recipes.

When cookies are cool, decorate with Decorating Icing (right), white or tinted. Using a waxed paper cone or a decorating tube fitted with a writing tip, fill in the features or outline the shapes made by the cutters. If desired, decorate with silver dragées.

With beaded dressmakers' pins, attach cookies to a styrofoam cone. (The one pictured on the opposite page is 12 inches tall and 7 inches in diameter at the base.) Start the pinning with the bottom row of cookies; then move to the row above, arranging the cookies so they overlap slightly.

To make the tree more festive, fill in spaces with little red bows and holly leaves. Split red Hall Sheen ribbon into narrow strips and make bow loops. Cut holly leaves from green Hall Sheen ribbon and stick onto the underside of the bow at an angle. Attach the decorations to the tree with dressmakers' pins.

NOTE: You can also use these cookies as decorations on a tabletop Christmas tree. Thread ribbon through the holes and tie cookies onto the branches.

CHOCOLATE GINGERBREAD COOKIES

    ½ cup butter, softened
    ¾ cup sugar
    1 egg
    ½ cup unsulphured dark molasses
    3 cups flour
    2 tablespoons cocoa
    1 teaspoon cinnamon
    1 teaspoon baking soda
    1 teaspoon salt
    ½ teaspoon baking powder

Cream butter; gradually add sugar, beating until light and fluffy. Beat in egg, then molasses. Sift together remaining ingredients and stir in, mixing until well blended. Chill 1 hour.

On a floured surface, roll out dough until 3/16 inch thick. Cut with cookie cutters and place on a greased baking sheet. Bake in a preheated 350° oven 7 minutes. Remove from sheet immediately and cool on a wire rack. Decorate as desired.

About 4 dozen 2-inch cookies or 2 dozen large cookies.

DECORATING ICING

    2 cups confectioners' sugar
    1 egg white, lightly beaten
       Food coloring (optional)

Mix sugar and a spoonful of egg white in a small bowl; beat until smooth, gradually adding more egg white to reach the desired consistency. Beat in coloring as desired.

To use, fill a waxed paper cone or a decorating tube fitted with a writing tip with some of the icing. This icing is ideal for outlining cookies or for "drawing" features and designs of your own.

About 1 cup.

NOTE: This icing can become stiff very quickly so make only one batch at a time and keep bowl covered with a damp cloth.

CHRISTMAS SUGAR COOKIES

¾ cup butter, softened
1 cup sugar
1 egg
2 cups flour
1 teaspoon baking powder
½ teaspoon salt
⅛ teaspoon ground nutmeg
2 tablespoons milk
1 teaspoon vanilla

Cream butter; gradually add sugar, beating until light and fluffy. Beat in egg. Sift together flour, baking powder, salt and nutmeg; add to creamed mixture alternately with milk and vanilla to form a stiff dough. Wrap in waxed paper and chill 1 hour.

On a floured surface, roll out the dough until 3/16 inch thick. Cut into desired shapes with holiday cookie cutters and place on an ungreased baking sheet. Bake in a preheated 400° oven 6 to 8 minutes or until golden. Remove to wire rack to cool. If desired, decorate with Decorating Icing (page 55).

About 3 dozen cookies.

NUTTED THIMBLE COOKIES

½ cup butter
⅓ cup sugar
1 egg, separated
½ teaspoon vanilla
1 cup flour
¼ teaspoon salt
½ cup finely chopped walnuts, pecans or hazelnuts
¼ cup raspberry or strawberry jam

Cream butter; gradually add sugar, beating until fluffy. Beat in egg yolk and vanilla. Sift in flour and salt, mixing to form a dough. Chill at least 1 hour.

With palms of hands, roll dough into 1-inch balls. Roll in slightly beaten egg white and then in chopped nuts. Place on a lightly greased baking sheet and press an indentation into each cookie with a thimble or your thumb. Fill each indentation with jam. Bake in a preheated 375° oven 13 to 15 minutes. Remove from sheet and cool on wire rack.

About 30 cookies.

FLORENTINES

½ cup sugar
½ cup heavy cream
3 tablespoons butter
1½ cups finely chopped blanched almonds
½ cup finely chopped candied orange peel
⅓ cup flour
4 ounces semisweet chocolate, melted

Combine sugar, cream and butter in a heavy saucepan; bring to a boil. Remove from heat and stir in almonds, orange peel and flour. Drop mixture by teaspoonfuls 3 inches apart onto a greased and floured baking sheet.

Bake in a preheated 350° oven about 10 minutes or until golden brown. Let cool on baking sheet 5 minutes before removing to wire rack to continue cooling. When completely cool, spread melted chocolate over bottom of each cookie. Let stand until chocolate hardens.

About 30 cookies.

WALNUT CRESCENTS

½ cup butter, softened
½ cup granulated sugar
½ cup finely ground walnuts
1 cup flour
⅛ teaspoon salt
1 teaspoon vanilla
  Confectioners' sugar

Cream butter; gradually add sugar, beating until light. Add nuts, flour, salt and vanilla; mix until dough holds together (if necessary, add 1 or 2 teaspoons cold water).

Using about 1 teaspoonful dough for each cookie, shape between palms of the hands into a roll about 2½ inches long, tapering at both ends. Bend the cookies into crescents and place on an ungreased baking sheet. Bake in a preheated 300° oven 20 to 25 minutes or until cookies are lightly browned and done inside (break one open to check). While still warm, dust heavily with confectioners' sugar and allow to cool to room temperature.

About 50 cookies.

Bar cookies travel well, so these would make a good long-distance present. Pack close together in a gift box, using waxed paper between the layers.

CRANBERRY BARS

CRANBERRY FILLING

¾ cup sugar
½ cup water
2 cups fresh cranberries, rinsed and picked over
¼ cup orange juice
1 tablespoon grated orange peel
1 tablespoon butter
½ teaspoon cinnamon
¼ teaspoon salt
1 cup walnuts, chopped

OATMEAL DOUGH

2 cups sifted flour
1 teaspoon salt
1½ cups sugar
1¼ cups butter, softened
3 cups uncooked oatmeal

To make cranberry filling, combine sugar and water in a heavy saucepan and bring to a boil. Add cranberries and cook until cranberries pop, about 5 minutes. Add orange juice, peel, butter, cinnamon and salt and cook another 5 minutes or until mixture thickens. Remove from heat and stir in walnuts. Set aside to cool.

To make oatmeal dough, sift together flour, salt and sugar; cut in butter with a pastry blender or fork until mixture resembles coarse meal. Add oatmeal and mix thoroughly.

Pat half the oatmeal dough in an ungreased 13x9x2-inch baking pan (or in two 8-inch square pans), patting in firmly and evenly. Spread cranberry filling on top, then pat the remaining oatmeal dough evenly on top. Bake in a preheated 425° oven 25 to 30 minutes or until lightly browned. Cool and cut into 1x3-inch bars.

About 40 bars.

KISSES

2 egg whites
¼ teaspoon salt
⅛ teaspoon cream of tartar
½ cup granulated sugar
3 tablespoons confectioners' sugar
2 ounces semisweet chocolate, grated
½ cup finely chopped hazelnuts or almonds

Beat egg whites until foamy. Add salt and cream of tartar and beat until soft peaks form. Sift sugars together; add about 2 tablespoons at a time, beating until stiff peaks form. Carefully fold in chocolate and nuts — do not overmix or meringue will fall.

With a pastry bag, pipe meringue into small kisses or drop by teaspoonfuls onto a lightly greased baking sheet. Bake in a preheated 250° oven 45 minutes or until set and dry.

About 50 kisses.

VARIATIONS: Substitute diced candied fruits for the chocolate, grated coconut for the nuts.

CARAMEL PISTACHIO CHEWS

1 cup dark corn syrup
1 cup sugar
½ cup butter
1 cup heavy cream
1 cup shelled pistachios, coarsely chopped

Combine corn syrup, sugar, butter and ½ cup of the cream in a heavy saucepan. Cook over low heat, stirring, until mixture boils. Raise heat to moderate and boil, stirring constantly, until a candy thermometer dipped in the syrup registers 240°. Remove from heat and slowly add remaining cream, stirring constantly. Return to heat and cook to 245°. Immediately pour into a buttered pan.

When cool enough to handle, turn caramel onto a buttered baking sheet. Working quickly, cut off a bite-size piece and roll it between the buttered palms of your hands, then roll in nuts, pressing nuts into caramel. Repeat, cutting and rolling piece by piece. If caramel becomes too hard to work, warm in a 250° oven a minute or two to soften.

About 40 candies.

GLACE PEELS, FRUITS AND NUTS

    2 cups sugar
    ½ cup light corn syrup
    1 cup water
       Pinch of salt
       Fruits and nuts (see note)

Combine sugar, corn syrup, water and salt in a small heavy saucepan. Place over moderate heat and stir constantly until mixture begins to boil. Cook without stirring to 280° on a candy thermometer; reduce heat and cook to 300°. As crystals collect on side of pan, wipe them away with a slightly wet pastry brush. Place pan in a larger saucepan of boiling water to keep from hardening as you work.

Drop fruit pieces or nuts one at a time into the syrup; lift out with a fork and hold over the saucepan, allowing any excess syrup to drain off. Invert fork over an oiled baking pan, placing each coated piece on the oiled surface. Allow to cool and harden in a dry spot. If desired, dip cooled glacé fruits or nuts into warm melted semisweet chocolate; place on waxed paper to cool and harden.

About 2 dozen candies.

NOTE: Try parboiled strips of orange peel, any dried fruits, fresh orange slices with peel, pineapple slices, whole cranberries, walnuts, pecans. Don't be afraid to experiment.

CHOCOLATE TRUFFLES

    6 ounces unsweetened chocolate
    ½ cup butter
    1 cup confectioners' sugar
    ¼ cup ground almonds or hazelnuts
    2 tablespoons heavy cream
       Cocoa powder

Melt chocolate and butter in the top of a double boiler over hot water, stirring until smooth. Remove from heat. Stir in sugar, nuts and cream and beat until smooth. Pour into a glass bowl and chill until firm enough to mold. Form into ½-inch balls and roll in cocoa.

About 3 dozen candies.

BOURBON BALLS

    2½ cups crushed vanilla wafers
    ⅓   cup bourbon
    ½   cup honey
    1   pound pecans, ground
        Confectioners' sugar

Combine crushed wafers, bourbon, honey and pecans in a bowl and mix thoroughly. Shape into balls with a 1-tablespoon measure. Roll balls in confectioners' sugar. Store in a covered container to ripen for a few days before using.

About 4½ dozen candies.

ROCKY ROAD

    6 ounces miniature marshmallows
    1 cup walnut pieces
    2 packages (6 ounces each) semisweet
       chocolate bits

Combine marshmallows and nuts and sprinkle evenly over the bottom of a buttered 8-inch square pan. Melt chocolate in the top of a double boiler over hot water, stirring frequently. Pour the melted chocolate evenly over marshmallow-nut mixture. Cool until firmly set and cut into 1-inch squares.

64 candies.

HOLIDAY NIBBLE MIX

    1 cup shelled almonds
    1 cup pecan halves
    1 cup walnut pieces
    ½ cup raisins
    ½ cup diced mixed candied fruits

Toss all ingredients to mix evenly. Store in tightly covered containers. Serve in small bowls.

4 cups.

At right — Christmas means the sight and aroma of homemade cookies and candies, packed for special gifts and set out for family sampling.

Be sure to make these at least a month in advance — and 4 months in advance is not too soon if you keep them well wrapped and moisten them weekly.

AGED FRUITCAKES

    1   cup plus 2 tablespoons butter
    1   cup plus 2 tablespoons brown sugar
    6   eggs, beaten
    3   cups flour
    2   teaspoons baking powder
    ½   teaspoon salt
    1   teaspoon cinnamon
    ½   teaspoon ground ginger
    ½   teaspoon ground nutmeg
    2½ cups currants
    2   cups dark raisins
    1   cup light raisins
    ½   cup glacé cherries, cut up
    ½   cup cut-up candied citrus peel
    1   cup walnuts or pecans, coarsely chopped
    ½   cup ground almonds
    2   teaspoons finely grated lemon peel
    3   tablespoons brandy
        Brandy, rum or sherry for aging

Line two 9x5x3-inch loaf pans with waxed paper; carefully grease and flour the paper. In a large bowl, cream butter; add sugar gradually, beating until light and creamy. Gradually beat in eggs. Sift together flour, baking powder, salt and spices and stir into the creamed mixture, ⅓ at a time. Combine fruits, nuts and lemon peel and mix in along with the 3 tablespoons brandy.

Divide mixture evenly between the loaf pans. Bake in a preheated 300° oven 2½ hours or until a metal skewer inserted into the center of each cake comes out clean. (Check the cakes after 1½ hours. If they are getting too dark, cover with brown paper.)

Remove fruitcakes from pans and cool on a wire rack. When still slightly warm, gently pierce tops with a skewer or fork and sprinkle with 1 to 2 tablespoons brandy, rum or sherry. When fruitcakes are cool, wrap each one in cheesecloth moistened with brandy, rum or sherry; then wrap in foil. Keep in a cool place in tightly covered tins. Check the cakes every week and sprinkle on a few tablespoons of brandy, rum or sherry, making sure the cheesecloth remains slightly damp. Before giving as a present, remove cheesecloth and wrap in plastic wrap.

LAST-MINUTE FRUITCAKE

    1   cup raisins
    1   cup maraschino cherries, halved
    1   cup cut-up pitted dates
    1   cup blanched almonds
    2   cups walnut pieces
    ¾   cup flour
    ¼   teaspoon baking soda
    ¼   teaspoon baking powder
    ½   teaspoon salt
    ¾   cup sugar
    3   eggs
    1   teaspoon vanilla

Lightly grease a 9x5x3-inch loaf pan. Line with waxed paper and grease the paper. Mix fruits and nuts in a large mixing bowl. Sift flour, baking soda, baking powder, salt and sugar over mixture; toss to coat all fruits and nuts with flour.

Beat eggs until foamy, then add vanilla. Pour over fruit mixture and stir just until blended. Pour into prepared loaf pan. Bake in a preheated 300° oven about 1½ hours. Remove from pan and cool on wire rack.

NOTE: For Fruitcake Gems, bake in muffin tins or small brioche molds. When cool, wrap individually in cellophane and tie with ribbon. (15 to 20 "gems.")

 ENTERTAINING IDEAS

A cookie exchange party is a fun way for you and your friends to acquire a variety of goodies and good recipes for the holidays. On the invitation ask each guest to bring a platter of cookies, the number to be determined by how many people are invited and how many cookies each guest exchanges.

When decorating for Christmas, don't overlook the kitchen. Suspend a favorite ornament in a window, add holiday bows to houseplants and keep containers filled with peppermints on the counters.

Make Christmas food part of your decorations with an old-fashioned Christmas tree. Hang decorated cookies with bows of yarn and ribbon and string garlands of popcorn and cranberries.

This recipe is so easy yet so special you'll want to make several batches. For gift giving, use decorative jars and perky bows.

CHOCOLATE-RUM-RAISIN SAUCE

12 ounces semisweet chocolate
2 cups raisins
1 cup dark rum

Combine chocolate, raisins and rum in the top of a double boiler over very low heat and cook, stirring, until chocolate melts. Pour into clean jars and cap tightly; store in a cool place. To use, reheat gently and serve over ice cream or unfrosted cake.

About 2 cups.

Use the gift tags to tell your friends how to serve this spirited fruit mixture.

CHRISTMAS VINTAGE CUP

1 cup dried apricots
1 cup dried pears
2 cups raisins
2 cups drained preserved kumquats
1 cup blanched almonds
1 cup sugar
2 to 3 cups port, sherry or brandy

Sterilize 4 glass 1-pint jars in boiling water (decorative apothecary jars make very attractive holiday gift containers). Fill each jar with alternating layers of apricots, pears, raisins, kumquats and almonds, sprinkling each layer with a little sugar. Repeat layers until jars are filled to within 1 inch of the top. Fill with wine or brandy to cover; seal tightly. Let stand in a cool place for at least 4 days to age. Fruit will absorb the liquid, so add more as needed to keep the fruit covered. Serve alone as a dessert or as a topping for ice cream or pudding.

About 2 quarts.

This traditional English sweet is usually used as a filling for pastry tarts or layer cakes, but it can also be used as a spread for breakfast rolls.

LEMON CURD

6 large lemons
6 eggs
¾ cup butter
3 cups sugar

Remove a thin strip of peel from one of the lemons and reserve. Cut lemons in half; squeeze juice and strain. Beat eggs and strain. Combine lemon juice, eggs, butter, sugar and reserved lemon peel in the top of a double boiler over simmering water; stir until the mixture thickens. Remove from heat and let cool. (It will continue to thicken as it cools.)

Remove peel and pour into sterilized jars. Seal at once and label; store in the refrigerator.

About 4½ cups.

Ceramic coffee mugs make good containers for these zesty spreads — nice gifts, too.

BRANDIED CHEESE CROCK

1 cup grated Cheddar cheese
¾ cup crumbled blue cheese
¾ cup butter
1 teaspoon prepared mustard
⅛ teaspoon ground nutmeg
3 tablespoons brandy

Allow cheeses and butter to stand at room temperature until softened. Blend in remaining ingredients until smooth. Pack into a 2½-cup crock; cover and refrigerate overnight before using. Serve with crisp crackers, toast or celery.

2½ cups.

VARIATIONS: Instead of using brandy, flavor the cheese with port, sherry or bourbon. For extra spiciness, add Worcestershire and hot pepper sauce. Or substitute cream cheese for all or part of the butter and add chopped walnuts for texture. For a totally different taste treat, use a mild cheese such as Fontina instead of blue cheese, and add a tablespoon or two of caraway or cumin seeds.

A good choice for friends who like to bake pies.

LEMON MINCEMEAT

   3 lemons
   3 tart green apples, cored and diced
   3 red apples, cored and diced
   1 pound dried apricots or pears
   3 cups (1 pound) dark raisins
   3 cups (1 pound) light raisins
  ¼ pound candied orange peel
1½ pounds grapes, cut up and seeded
1½ cups almonds, blanched and slivered
4½ cups sugar
1½ cups brandy

Remove peel from lemons and reserve. Cut lemons in half and squeeze; strain juice and reserve. Put lemon peel, apples, dried apricots, raisins and candied orange peel through a large-holed food chopper. Add lemon juice, grapes, almonds, sugar and brandy; mix well. Cover and let stand at least 1 hour, stirring occasionally. Pour into sterilized jars and cover; label, then store in a cool, dark place.

3 quarts.

HERBED MUSTARD

  ½ cup dry mustard
  2 tablespoons brown sugar
     Pinch of salt
  6 tablespoons white wine
  ¼ cup white wine vinegar
  2 egg yolks
  ¾ cup oil
  ¼ teaspoon tarragon

Mix mustard, sugar and salt. Blend in wine and vinegar, stirring to make a smooth paste. Beat in egg yolks; then slowly beat in oil, a few drops at a time, until smooth and creamy. Stir in tarragon. Spoon into small jars and cover tightly. Refrigerate overnight or longer before using.

About 1½ cups.

VARIATIONS: Instead of tarragon, use other dried herbs and spices such as basil, marjoram, oregano, parsley, rosemary, sage, thyme or crushed green peppercorns. For the white wine, you can substitute sherry, gin, scotch, cider vinegar or tarragon vinegar.

A truly individual touch. Pack in attractive jars or tightly covered metal gift boxes.

FLAVORED TEAS

Teas flavored with herbs and spices make unusual and refreshing beverages. Simply mix tea leaves with dried herbs and spices (use about 1 teaspoon for each tablespoon tea leaves). The following are particularly good combinations:

With dark, smoky teas, such as Lapsang souchong: mint, bergamot, camomile.

With black teas, such as Darjeeling or orange pekoe: dried orange peel, broken cinnamon sticks, cloves.

With oolong teas: anise seeds, thyme, sage.

With green teas: rose petals, sassafras.

Make these vinegars when the fresh herbs are available, then store them for the holidays.

HERBED VINEGARS

Flavored vinegars may be made with distilled white vinegar, cider or malt vinegars, or wine vinegars. Wine vinegars are lighter and milder in flavor, while cider vinegars are strong and full-bodied. You simply add a fresh herb, such as tarragon or savory, or a combination of herbs to the vinegar of your choice; cover lightly and keep at room temperature for at least 10 days but no more than 4 weeks. Then strain through cheesecloth and store the vinegar in tightly capped bottles. Follow these tips:

Use no more than 3 tablespoons fresh herbs per quart of vinegar.

For best results, use fresh herbs. Dried herbs limit the keeping quality of vinegar; if you use them, make the vinegar in very small batches for use within a few days. Figure on 1 tablespoon dried herbs per quart of vinegar.

At right—A colorful selection of gifts from the kitchen, ready and waiting to greet the holiday season. Enjoy the making as well as the giving.

BRANDIED PEACHES

4 pounds small firm peaches (clingstone)
4 cups sugar
1 pint brandy

Drop peaches into boiling water and simmer 3 to 4 minutes, then plunge into cold water. To peel, release skin at the stem end with the point of a knife; pull edge of skin and the rest of it will peel off.

Bring 1 quart water and the sugar to a boil in a large saucepan. Add only a few peaches at a time and simmer 5 to 10 minutes or until tender. Remove peaches with a slotted spoon and pack into hot sterilized jars. Repeat until all peaches are cooked.

Boil syrup to thicken slightly and stir in brandy. Pour boiling syrup over peaches to within ¼ inch of top of jar. Wipe rims and seal. Cool, check seals and label. Store in a cool, dark place.

4 pints.

PICKLED PEARS

6 pounds small firm ripe pears
Whole cloves
1 tablespoon salt
1 tablespoon white vinegar
4 cups sugar
2 cups water
2 cups cider vinegar
6 one-inch pieces cinnamon sticks

Peel pears, leaving stems intact. Stick a clove into the base of each pear. To prevent discoloration, place pears in a bowl of cold water to which the salt and white vinegar have been added.

Combine sugar, 2 cups water and the cider vinegar in a large saucepan and bring to a boil. Add ⅓ of the pears and simmer 7 to 10 minutes or until tender. Remove with a slotted spoon and pack tightly into hot sterilized jars. Repeat two more times.

Place a piece of cinnamon stick in each jar. Pour boiling syrup over pears to within 1 inch of top of jar. Wipe rims and seal. Cool, check seals and label. Store in a cool, dark place.

6 pints.

Quinces, which resemble large yellow apples, are plentiful in autumn. They're very tart, however, so the jelly calls for plenty of sugar.

QUINCE JELLY

3 pounds quinces
3 cups sugar

Slice quinces and measure. Place in a saucepan and add 1½ cups water for every 2 cups of fruit. Simmer 45 minutes. Drain through a wet jelly bag. When the bag stops dripping, discard the pulp.

Measure juice and, if necessary, add water to make 4 cups. Add sugar and stir until dissolved. Simmer until a candy thermometer placed in the jelly registers 220° (or test by placing a few drops on a cold plate; if they jell, the jelly is done).

Pour into hot sterilized jars. Wipe rims and seal. Cool, check seals and label. Store in a cool, dark place.

2 pints.

STRAWBERRY OR BLUEBERRY PRESERVES

6 cups strawberries or blueberries
6 cups sugar
2 tablespoons lemon juice

Wash and hull strawberries, or wash and pick over blueberries. Add sugar and allow to stand at least 2 hours or overnight. Stir in lemon juice. Bring to a boil, stirring to dissolve sugar. Simmer for about 15 minutes. The preserves are done when a candy thermometer reads 220° (or test by placing a few drops on a cold plate; if they jell, the preserves are done).

Remove from heat and skim foam. Allow to cool 20 minutes; skim and stir occasionally. Pour into hot sterilized jars or glasses. Cover with melted paraffin or seal while hot; label. Store in a cool, dark place.

4 to 5 eight-ounce jars.

RING IN THE NEW

*Whether you celebrate it as the finale of the old
or the kickoff for the new, New Year's is the perfect time to
entertain friends. It's easy, so enjoy yourself.*

Cheer the New Year in with an array of exciting dishes — a wealth of appetizers, a flavorful punch and something on the sweet side for a touch of dessert. Do as much as you can in advance (see page 69), then relax and ring in the new.

CHEESE BOARD
QUICK SHRIMP QUICHE
SWEET-N-SOUR TURKEY BITES
MINI CREPES   SOUFFLE MUSHROOMS
PHYLLO MEAT PIE
BACON AND EGG ROULADE
CRANBERRY PUNCH
COLD EGGNOG SOUFFLE

CHEESE BOARD

Few foods are as popular on buffet tables or with cocktails as cheese, and an attractively arranged cheese board is a special pleasure on New Year's Eve. Keep these pointers in mind when planning your party:

Serve a variety of cheeses. Your guests' tastes will differ, so you should offer 3 or 4 choices to satisfy everyone. Consider serving one mild cheese, such as Port Salut, Bel Paese or Edam; one Swiss-type cheese, such as Emmenthal, Gruyère or Appenzell; one soft-ripened cheese, such as Brie or Camembert; and one blue cheese, such as Roquefort, Stilton or domestic blue. Other possibilities include Cheddars and spiced or flavored cheese.

Avoid overdecorating the cheese board. Few things are more naturally beautiful than good cheese on plain wood. And don't crowd the board. Leave enough room between cheeses for cutting. And be sure to supply enough knives or cutters.

For a menu such as this, with many other appetizers offered in addition to the cheese, buy enough for 2 to 3 ounces per person.

Offer 2 or 3 kinds of breads and crackers with the cheese. And a bowl of grapes or pears and crisp apples is a welcome accompaniment.

QUICK SHRIMP QUICHE

  1 **package refrigerated crescent dinner rolls**
  1 **pound raw shrimp, shelled and deveined, or**
      1 package (6 ounces) tiny frozen shrimp
12 **very thin slices pepperoni, shredded**
  2 **tablepoons butter**
  1 **pimiento, slivered**
1½ **cups grated Swiss cheese**
  4 **eggs**
1¾ **cups light cream**
      Pinch each of salt, pepper and dry mustard

Grease a 13x9x2-inch baking dish and cover bottom and sides with rectangles of crescent dough, pressing firmly to seal all seams.

Sauté shrimp and pepperoni lightly in butter; add pimiento. Sprinkle grated cheese on crescent dough crust. Top with shrimp mixture. Beat eggs with remaining ingredients; pour over filling in crust.

Bake in a preheated 400° oven 10 minutes. Reduce heat to 325° and bake about 30 minutes or until custard is set. To serve, cut into small squares.

About 24 appetizers.

SWEET-N-SOUR TURKEY BITES

SAUCE

- 1 cup chicken broth
- 1 cup pineapple juice
- ½ cup sugar
- ⅓ cup red wine vinegar
- 2 teaspoons soy sauce
- 2 tablespoons cornstarch

TURKEY BITES

- 2 pounds ground raw turkey meat
- 2 eggs, beaten
- 1 cup dry bread crumbs
- 1 teaspoon salt
- ½ teaspoon pepper
- 2 tablespoons butter
- 2 teaspoons oil

Combine sauce ingredients in a large saucepan. Stir to dissolve sugar and cornstarch. Bring to a boil, stirring, until sauce becomes clear. Cook 1 minute.

Lightly mix turkey, eggs, bread crumbs, salt and pepper. Shape into small uniform-size balls. Heat butter and oil in a skillet and sauté turkey bites, a few at a time. Add them to the sauce and simmer 15 minutes. (Or place sautéed turkey bites in a casserole, add sauce and bake, uncovered, in a preheated 350° oven 20 minutes.)

About 70 appetizers.

NOTE: Look for preground turkey meat, sold in frozen rolls; or buy a boned 2-pound turkey breast and put through a meat grinder or food processor.

MINI CREPES

- 4 eggs
- 4 egg yolks
- 2¼ cups milk
- ¼ cup brandy
- 2 cups sifted flour
- 1 teaspoon salt
- ¼ cup butter, melted

Beat whole eggs, egg yolks, milk and brandy. Add flour and salt and beat until smooth. Stir in butter and let batter stand 30 minutes at room temperature (or longer in refrigerator).

Lightly grease a heated 4-inch skillet or crepe pan. Stir batter and pour about 1 tablespoon into center of pan; immediately tilt pan to spread the batter evenly over bottom. Cook about 30 seconds over moderate heat, just until bottom is lightly browned. Turn and cook other side 15 to 20 seconds longer. Stack finished crepes on a flat surface; cover with a piece of waxed paper or a clean cloth. Choose from the fillings below (each recipe fills 10 crepes) and roll up as directed.

About 50 mini crepes.

ASPARAGUS-HOLLANDAISE CREPES

- 3 tablespoons hollandaise sauce
- 2 teaspoons lemon juice
- 10 fresh or frozen asparagus spears, cooked and cooled

SHRIMP CREPES

- 1 cup chopped cooked shrimp
- ¼ cup mayonnaise
- ⅛ teaspoon salt

GOUDA CREPES

- 1 cup grated Gouda cheese
- 3 tablespoons Dijon-style mustard

SMOKED SALMON OR KIPPER CREPES

- 6 ounces smoked salmon or kippers, diced
- 1 package (3 ounces) cream cheese, softened
- 2 teaspoons chopped chives

CHICKEN CREPES

- 1 cup minced cooked chicken
- ¼ cup mayonnaise
- 1 tablespoon chopped fresh parsley or 1 teaspoon dried parsley flakes

For Asparagus-Hollandaise Crepes, spread each of 10 crepes with some of the hollandaise and sprinkle with a few drops of lemon juice. Place an asparagus spear toward the lower edge of each crepe and roll up from bottom.

For each of the remaining fillings, mix ingredients together. Divide each mixture among 10 crepes, placing filling toward the lower edge, and roll up from bottom.

50 appetizers.

SOUFFLE MUSHROOMS

1 cup grated Swiss cheese
1 cup soft bread crumbs
4 eggs, separated
1 cup milk
32 large mushrooms, of uniform size
4 tablespoons butter
¼ teaspoon salt
Pinch of pepper

Toss grated cheese with bread crumbs. Beat egg yolks and milk; pour over crumbs. Wipe mushrooms and remove stems. Chop enough stems to make 1 cup and sauté briefly in 2 tablespoons of the butter. Stir into bread crumbs along with the salt and pepper.

Beat egg whites until stiff; fold into mixture. Melt remaining butter and gently dip in mushroom caps. Pile filling into caps and arrange on a greased baking sheet. Bake in a preheated 400° oven 10 to 12 minutes or until filling is golden. Serve at once.

32 appetizers.

PHYLLO MEAT PIE

1 pound ground beef or lamb
2 tablespoons butter or olive oil
1 medium onion, minced
2 cloves garlic, minced
¼ cup dry red wine
1 tablespoon tomato paste
1 teaspoon dried parsley flakes
½ teaspoon oregano
1 teaspoon salt
¼ teaspoon pepper
⅛ teaspoon cinnamon
¼ cup grated Parmesan cheese
½ pound (10 to 12 sheets) phyllo dough
1 cup butter, melted

Cook ground meat in butter until lightly browned, breaking up meat with a fork as it cooks. With a slotted spoon, transfer meat to a bowl and discard all but 2 tablespoons fat from the skillet. Cook onion and garlic in remaining fat until onion is soft. Add wine, tomato paste and seasonings and stir to blend well, cooking 2 to 3 minutes longer. Add to meat mixture and mix well. Let cool for 10 minutes, then stir in cheese.

Carefully unroll phyllo dough and cut sheets in half to form 12x8-inch sheets. Place one sheet in bottom of a greased 12x8x2-inch baking pan and brush with melted butter; lay another sheet on top and brush again. Continue until there are 10 to 12 sheets in the pan, each brushed with melted butter. Spread meat mixture evenly over phyllo dough. Continue to layer remaining sheets of dough over the meat, brushing each with melted butter.

Bake in a preheated 350° oven 1 hour or until top is crisp and golden. Cut into 2-inch squares, then cut each square into 2 triangles. Serve hot.

48 appetizers.

BACON AND EGG ROULADE

6 tablespoons butter
¾ cup flour
1 teaspoon salt
Pinch of paprika
3 cups milk
6 eggs, separated
1 pound bacon
1 large sweet onion, thinly sliced
1 cup grated Cheddar cheese

Melt butter in a heavy-bottomed saucepan. Add flour, salt and paprika; stir to combine. Gradually add milk, stirring until smooth. Cook over low heat, stirring often, about 4 minutes or until thick. Remove from heat and blend in egg yolks. Beat egg whites until stiff and fold into mixture. Line a 15x10-inch jelly roll pan with waxed paper; grease and flour the paper. Pour batter into pan. Bake in a preheated 325° oven 40 minutes or until golden.

Meanwhile, cook bacon in a skillet until crisp. Drain and crumble. Pour off all but 1 tablespoon drippings; add onion and sauté until soft.

Cool roulade slightly and turn out onto another sheet of waxed paper. Cover with cheese, then sprinkle on bacon and onion. Roll up from the long side. Remove to a platter and cut into ¾-inch slices.

About 20 appetizers.

68

CRANBERRY PUNCH

1   can (20 ounces) pineapple rings
½   cup whole cranberries
1   quart cranberry juice
1   quart apple juice
    Juice of 2 lemons
1   quart bourbon or blended whiskey
1   quart club soda

Drain pineapple, reserving juice. Arrange pineapple rings and cranberries in a 1½-quart ring mold. Add ¼ inch water and freeze solid. Remove from freezer and add just enough water to cover fruits; freeze again. Then add water to fill mold and freeze until ready to serve.

Combine reserved pineapple juice with remaining juices and liquor and chill until ready to serve. Just before serving turn out ice ring into punch bowl and pour in juice mixture. Add club soda and stir gently.

About 35 servings (4 ounces each).

COLD EGGNOG SOUFFLE

8   eggs
2   envelopes gelatin
1½   cups sugar
1½   cups milk
    Pinch of salt
½   cup rum or bourbon
2   teaspoons vanilla
⅛   teaspoon ground nutmeg
4   egg whites
2   cups heavy cream, whipped
    Additional nutmeg for garnish

Separate egg yolks from whites and beat yolks lightly. Stir gelatin into ½ cup of the sugar. Using a whisk, beat egg yolks, milk, salt and sugar-gelatin mixture in the top of a double boiler, over simmering water, until custard thickens enough to coat a spoon. Do not overcook or yolks will curdle. Add liquor and cook, stirring, until mixture thickens and coats spoon again. Stir in vanilla and nutmeg. Chill, stirring often, until custard mixture mounds in a spoon, about 1 hour.

Beat the 12 egg whites until thick. Gradually beat in remaining sugar, and beat until meringue is stiff but not dry. Fold into custard sauce in a large bowl. Fold in whipped cream.

Lightly butter a band of waxed paper or foil and fasten around a 2-quart soufflé dish to form a collar extending 1 or 2 inches over the top of the dish. Pour in soufflé mixture and sprinkle with nutmeg. Chill until firm, 2 to 4 hours. Before serving, carefully remove collar.

About 20 servings.

NOTE: Make this early in the day or the day before your party. Dessert will be ready and waiting, with no last-minute fuss! If custard mixture should set while chilling, beat until light before folding in beaten egg whites.

⏰ PLANNING AHEAD

Enjoy all the New Year's fun at your own party with these do-ahead appetizers. Cook ahead and join your guests. Here are some guidelines:
• A week or two ahead, make the Mini-Crepes and freeze them. They can be thawed, filled and then refrigerated the morning of the party. The Quick Shrimp Quiche can also be baked in advance and frozen. On the morning of the party, transfer it to the refrigerator to thaw, then pop it into a 400° oven to reheat for about 20 minutes before serving.
• A day or two ahead, you can begin making Sweet-N-Sour Turkey Bites, Phyllo Meat Pie and even Bacon and Egg Roulade. All of them will keep in the refrigerator for a day or two if well wrapped. Just before serving, reheat at 350°. And, of course, the Eggnog Soufflé is best if made early in the day or the day before.
• While the Soufflé Mushrooms have to wait to be cooked until just before serving, the base for the filling can be prepared ahead and refrigerated, ready to receive the beaten egg whites at the last minute.
• The ice ring for the punch bowl can be made a day in advance, but wait until the afternoon of the party to combine the juices and liquor.

BIRTHDAY MEMORIES

Birthdays are special holidays for everyone. Make every birthday celebration memorable with a spectacular cake and an outstanding dinner fit for any occasion.

A perfect choice for preschoolers.

TRAIN CAKE

2½ cups flour
1½ cups sugar
2½ teaspoons baking powder
¾ teaspoon salt
¾ cup butter, softened
3 eggs
¾ cup milk
1½ teaspoons vanilla
    Butter Icing (right)

FOR DECORATION

    Red and yellow food coloring
½ ounce semisweet chocolate, melted
20 gumdrop rings
8 gumdrops
⅓ cup semisweet chocolate bits

Sift flour, sugar, baking powder and salt into a mixing bowl. Add butter, eggs, milk and vanilla. With an electric mixer, beat at low speed 3 minutes, until batter is smooth.

Grease and flour 4 small loaf pans, each 5½x3¼ inches, and one 10-ounce can, such as a well-washed condensed soup can. Pour batter into pans and can, making a hollow in center so that finished cakes will be flat. Bake in a preheated 350° oven about 25 minutes or until top springs back when touched lightly. Cool in pans and can 10 minutes, then loosen sides and turn out onto cake racks to finish cooling.

Use round loaf for locomotive, 3 loaf cakes for cars and 1 loaf cake for coal car. Cut a 1-inch vertical slice from one end of the coal car loaf for locomotive cabin; hollow out top of coal car loaf, about 1 inch deep, for bin. Lay round loaf on its side and place reserved 1-inch slice on top at one end for cabin, using icing to hold it in place.

To color icing: Beat a few drops of yellow food coloring into half of the icing; set aside. Beat a few drops of red food coloring into half of the remaining icing; set aside. Add melted chocolate to the remaining icing and blend well.

Frost entire train, using chocolate for the locomotive, yellow for 3 cars and red for the coal car. Any extra chocolate or red icing may be used to decorate the yellow cars. Use gumdrop rings for wheels, 1 gumdrop for headlight and place 1 gumdrop on top of engine toward front and 2 gumdrops on top of each yellow car. Fill the hollow in the coal car with chocolate bits.

About 20 small servings.

BUTTER ICING

3 cups sifted confectioners' sugar
1½ cups (3 sticks) butter, softened
2 egg yolks
1 tablespoon vanilla

Combine all ingredients in a mixing bowl. With an electric mixer, beat at moderate speed until smooth, about 5 minutes.

About 3 cups.

NOTE: Before frosting the loaf cakes, brush off any loose crumbs from the sides and edges. With a spatula, lightly frost the sides to seal in crumbs. Then apply a heavier layer, stroking from the bottom up and building an edge at the top of the cake. Frost the top last, bringing the icing out to the built-up edge.

A little girl's delight. Served on a turntable, the ballerina will pirouette.

BALLERINA CAKE

2¼ cups flour
1½ cups sugar
  1 tablespoon baking powder
  1 teaspoon salt
½ cup vegetable oil
  5 eggs, separated
¾ cup orange juice
  2 egg whites
½ teaspoon cream of tartar
⅓ cup well-drained crushed pineapple
    Tutu Icing (below)
    Doll, about 8 inches tall

Sift flour, sugar, baking powder and salt into a mixing bowl. Add oil, egg yolks (5) and orange juice; stir until smooth.

In a large bowl, beat egg whites (7) with cream of tartar until stiff peaks form. Gently fold in egg yolk mixture just until blended and no white shows. Fold in crushed pineapple.

Pour batter into a greased and floured 10-inch Bundt pan. Bake in a preheated 325° oven about 1 hour or until top springs back when touched lightly. Remove from oven and cool in pan 15 minutes, then turn out onto a cake rack to finish cooling. Place cake on serving plate.

Wrap lower half of doll in plastic wrap to keep clean. Insert doll into hole in center of cake so that the cake forms a "skirt". Frost with Tutu Icing, using the tip of a spatula to create a "ruffled" look. Use icing to make a bodice on doll, filling in the space between the doll and the cake.

TUTU ICING

¼ cup light corn syrup
½ cup sugar
  2 tablespoons pineapple juice or water
  2 egg whites
    Yellow food coloring

Combine corn syrup, sugar and pineapple juice in a small saucepan. Cover and bring to boil. Uncover and continue to boil over medium heat until syrup registers 238° on a candy thermometer — the soft ball stage. (No thermometer? Drop a little of the mixture into very cold water; when removed, it will form a soft ball.)

Beat egg whites until stiff peaks form. Slowly pour hot syrup into the egg whites in a thin stream, beating constantly. Continue to beat until icing is stiff. Tint with yellow food coloring.

About 2 cups.

NOTE: All the birthday cakes on these pages freeze well and, with the exception of Tutu Icing, so do their icings. Unfrosted cakes can be wrapped and frozen as soon as they are cool; thaw in the wrapping. Frosted cakes should be frozen first, then wrapped for longer storage; thaw unwrapped.

 # ENTERTAINING IDEAS

Birthdays come but one a year, so plan to make the most of this very special day.

Adult Birthday Parties
Plan a memories party based on the year the honoree was born. Fill a scrapbook with vintage photographs and magazine and newspaper clippings from the year. Decorate with motifs from the era.

Teen-age Birthday Parties
For a party with an unusual look, stage a backwards party. Invitations instruct guests to come wearing their clothes backwards or inside out. Hold reverse games such as Backward Spelling Bee and serve food in reverse order, starting with ice cream.

Children's Birthday Parties
Have a circus party, complete with balloons and circus decorations. Ask a teen-ager to dress as a clown and assist with games and refreshments. Plan plenty of games and provide clown party hats and boxes of animal crackers to take home as favors. Relay races are an exciting way to start the party. Divide the children into two teams and line them up single file. Give the first child in each line a spoon with a marble in it. Each child must carry the spoon to a goal and back without dropping the marble. If it is dropped, the marble must be scooped up without using hands. The first team to finish wins.

A "healthy" cake to suit the taste of teens.

BANANA-NUT CAKE

½ cup butter
1¼ cups sugar
2 eggs
2⅓ cups flour
2½ teaspoons baking powder
½ teaspoon baking soda
½ teaspoon salt
½ teaspoon cinnamon
1 cup mashed ripe bananas (about 2 medium)
½ cup buttermilk
¼ teaspoon vanilla
¾ cup chopped walnuts
   Cream Cheese Icing (below)
   Food coloring

Cream butter and sugar until light and fluffy. Beat in eggs, one at a time.

Sift together flour, baking powder, baking soda, salt and cinnamon. Combine bananas, buttermilk and vanilla. Add dry ingredients to butter mixture alternately with banana mixture, stirring after each addition. Stir in ½ cup of the chopped nuts.

Pour batter into a greased and floured 9-inch tube pan. Bake in a preheated 350° oven about 50 minutes or until top springs back when touched lightly. Invert on a cake rack and cool completely before removing from pan.

Brush loose crumbs from cooled cake. Frost top and sides with Cream Cheese Icing, reserving ½ cup of the icing for decoration. Sprinkle remaining chopped nuts on top of cake, along inner and outer edges. Blend food coloring into reserved icing and, using a pastry tube fitted with a writing tip, write a birthday message on top of cake.

CREAM CHEESE ICING

2 packages (3 ounces each) cream cheese
1 tablespoon milk
1 teaspoon vanilla
   Pinch of salt
2½ cups sifted confectioners' sugar

Beat cheese, milk, vanilla and salt until light and fluffy. Gradually beat in sugar until smooth.

About 2½ cups.

For birthday boys and girls of all ages.

DOUBLE-RICH CHOCOLATE CAKE

1 cup butter
½ cup light brown sugar
2 cups granulated sugar
6 ounces unsweetened chocolate, melted
6 eggs
3¾ cups flour
¼ cup cornstarch
2½ teaspoons salt
2 teaspoons baking powder
1 teaspoon baking soda
1 cup plain yogurt
½ cup milk
2 teaspoons vanilla
   Rich Chocolate Icing (below)

Cream butter and sugars until light and fluffy. Stir in chocolate and mix well. Add eggs, one at a time, beating well after each addition.

Sift together flour, cornstarch, salt, baking powder and baking soda. Combine yogurt, milk, and vanilla. Add dry ingredients to chocolate mixture alternately with yogurt mixture.

Pour batter into 3 greased and floured 8-inch round cake pans. Bake in a preheated 325° oven 50 to 60 minutes or until a cake tester inserted in center comes out clean. Cool in pans 30 minutes, then turn out onto cake racks to finish cooling.

Brush loose crumbs from each cooled layer. Frost top of one layer with some of the Rich Chocolate Icing; top with a second layer and frost with more of the icing; add third layer. Frost top and sides of cake with remaining icing and decorate as desired.

RICH CHOCOLATE ICING

¼ cup heavy cream
8 ounces unsweetened chocolate, melted
2 cups sifted confectioners' sugar
4 eggs
5 tablespoons butter, softened

Beat cream, chocolate and sugar until well blended. Add eggs, one at a time, beating well after each addition. Beat in butter until smooth.

About 2 cups.

Marking a milestone? Any day that calls for a celebration calls for a dinner like this, with that most elegant of roasts, Beef Wellington. To add to the festivities, toast the event with a gala champagne punch. It's an extraordinary way to honor special occasions, from birthdays to anniversaries.

BEEF WELLINGTON

MADEIRA SAUCE

GLAZED CARROTS

BROCCOLI WITH LEMON SAUCE

GENOISE CAKE
WITH COFFEE BUTTER CREAM

SPECIAL CHAMPAGNE PUNCH

BEEF WELLINGTON

Quick Puff Pastry (right)
3-pound trimmed filet of beef
Salt and pepper
Vegetable oil
¼ **cup finely chopped fresh mushrooms**
1 **tablespoon butter**
1 **tablespoon brandy**
1 **cup Chopped Chicken Liver (page 43) or**
    liver pâté
1 **egg, beaten**

Early in the day or the day before, prepare Quick Puff Pastry.

Trim any fat from filet; season with salt and pepper and brush with oil. Place on a rack in a roasting pan and roast in a preheated 400° oven 30 minutes (for a rare roast). Remove from oven and cool to room temperature.

Cook chopped mushrooms in butter over high heat 1 minute, stirring once or twice. Add brandy and continue to cook until most of the liquid has evaporated. Remove from heat and add to chopped livers; mix well. Spread liver mixture on top of filet.

Roll pastry into a rectangle less than ¼ inch thick. Place filet, with the liver mixture underneath, lengthwise on pastry. Wrap pastry around filet, overlapping the edges to form a seam; moisten edges to seal. Trim top layer of pastry from ends and fold up over filet; moisten edges to seal.

Brush pastry with beaten egg. Decorate top with designs cut from scraps of pastry. Gently brush designs with remaining beaten egg. Carefully transfer wrapped filet to a lightly greased baking sheet. Bake in a preheated 450° oven about 25 minutes or until pastry is golden brown. Remove from oven and let stand in a warm place 10 minutes before carving. If desired, decorate serving platter with Mushroom Cap Garnish (page 77).

8 to 10 servings.

NOTE: You can partially cook the filet and wrap it in pastry early in the day. Bring to room temperature and bake about 25 minutes. For a shortcut version of Beef Wellington, use canned liver pâté for topping and frozen prepared puff pastry for dough.

QUICK PUFF PASTRY

¾ **cup (12 tablespoons) butter**
2 **cups flour**
1 **teaspoon salt**
6 **tablespoons water**

Soften half (6 tablespoons) of the butter in a mixing bowl. Add flour and blend thoroughly into butter. Add salt and water and knead lightly to make a dough. Form into a ball; cover and refrigerate 1 hour.

On a floured board, roll out the dough into a rectangle ¼ inch thick. Slightly soften remaining butter and spread over ⅔ of the rectangle, leaving a 1-inch unbuttered margin around the edges. Fold unbuttered third of dough over the center third; fold remaining third on top.

Turn dough 90 degrees and roll out into another rectangle about ⅓ inch thick. Fold into fourths as follows: First fold short ends of rectangle in to meet in center; then fold one half over the other, as if closing a book. Once again, turn dough 90 degrees and roll into rectangle and fold into fourths. Cover and refrigerate at least 1 hour. (The pastry can be made in advance and refrigerated up to 48 hours.)

Before using, roll into a rectangle and fold into fourths a third time. Then roll out to encase beef.

NOTE: If, at any stage, the folded dough becomes difficult to roll or if the butter seems to be getting too soft, refrigerate for about an hour.

Elegant Beef Wellington is not as difficult to make as you might think.

1. For the first folding of the dough, be sure to fold the unbuttered third over the center buttered third; fold the remaining buttered third on top.

2. For the second folding, bring the two ends in to meet in the center, then fold one half over the other.

3. When wrapping the filet, be careful not to stretch the dough. Overlap the edges to form a seam.

4. Before folding up the ends, trim off some of the top layer of pastry to reduce the bulk.

5. Use the tip of a knife to help position the pastry designs on top of the wrapped filet.

MADEIRA SAUCE

2 tablespoons butter
¼ cup minced carrots
¼ cup minced celery
¼ cup minced onion
2 tablespoons flour
2 cups brown beef broth
½ cup diced fresh or canned tomato
1 bay leaf
 Pinch of thyme
3 tablespoons Madeira wine
 Salt and pepper to taste
1 tablespoon butter

Heat 2 tablespoons butter in a heavy saucepan. Add carrots, celery and onion and cook, stirring once or twice, until vegetables just begin to brown. Stir in flour and continue to cook, stirring frequently, until well browned.

Bring broth to a boil and add to the vegetable mixture, stirring briskly. Add tomato, bay leaf and thyme and simmer gently 30 to 45 minutes, until reduced to about 1½ cups. Strain, pressing the vegetables to squeeze all their liquid into the sauce. Add Madeira, salt and pepper; return to a simmer. Remove from heat and swirl in 1 tablespoon butter. Serve immediately.

About 1½ cups.

MUSHROOM CAP GARNISH

10 large mushrooms
 Juice of ½ lemon
2 tablespoons butter
1 teaspoon salt

Cut off each mushroom stem flush with the edge of mushroom cap; do not pull stem out or the cap may collapse when cooked. Peel caps by loosening skin at outer edge and pulling off toward center. With a small, sharp knife, cut a large **X** about ⅛ inch deep in the peeled cap to mark the surface into quarters. Make designs by gently pressing the tip of the knife into caps to make **V**-shaped indentations.

Bring 2 cups water to a boil with lemon juice, butter and salt. Add mushrooms and cook 3 minutes; drain thoroughly.

GLAZED CARROTS

2 pounds carrots
3 tablespoons butter
2 tablespoons sugar
¼ cup apricot jam
 Salt to taste

Wash and scrape carrots; cut into diagonal slices. Cook, covered, in a small amount of boiling salted water until just tender, about 12 minutes (do not overcook). Drain.

Heat butter, sugar and apricot jam in a saucepan or skillet, stirring to combine. Add carrots and salt, stirring until carrots are coated. Cook over low heat, stirring gently, until carrots are evenly glazed, about 3 minutes.

8 to 10 servings (in this menu; fewer if served as the only vegetable).

BROCCOLI WITH LEMON SAUCE

2 bunches fresh broccoli (about 3 pounds)
6 tablespoons butter
6 tablespoons lemon juice

Remove tough ends of broccoli stalks and trim off coarse leaves. Wash well. If stalks are very thick, cut into serving-size lengthwise strips. Arrange broccoli in a large skillet or baking pan with stalk ends to the center and blossoms to the outside. Pour just enough boiling salted water over broccoli to cover stalks. Cover with hot damp kitchen towels and return to a boil. Cook 5 minutes, then carefully roll towels back from blossom ends so that only the stalks are covered. Cook just until tender, about 7 to 10 minutes longer. Drain.

Melt butter in a saucepan over medium heat; stir in lemon juice. Remove broccoli to a serving dish and top with sauce, or serve sauce separately.

8 to 10 servings (in this menu; fewer if served as the only vegetable).

NOTE: You'll find this new method of cooking broccoli, borrowed from a fine restaurant kitchen, greatly improves the eating quality of the cooked vegetable. No more soggy blossoms with too-tough stalks.

GENOISE CAKE WITH COFFEE BUTTER CREAM

6 eggs
¾ cup sugar (preferably extra-fine)
1 teaspoon vanilla
1 cup flour
¼ cup butter, melted
2 cups Coffee Butter Cream (right)

Preheat oven to 350°. Butter and flour two 8-inch round cake pans. The oven and pans must be ready as soon as the batter is mixed to ensure maximum rising.

Place eggs, sugar and vanilla in a mixing bowl. Set the bowl over a pot of simmering water — make sure the water does not touch the bowl. With a wire whisk or hand-held electric mixer, beat 1 or 2 minutes, just until the mixture is lukewarm. Remove from heat immediately. Using an electric mixer, beat at high speed until the mixture is pale yellow, has tripled in volume and forms a thick ribbon when dropped from a spoon.

Gradually sift flour into beaten eggs, folding in gently but thoroughly. Drizzle in butter, again folding in gently but thoroughly. (Do not use any of the milky liquid that may have settled at the bottom of melted butter.) The entire folding process should be done as quickly and carefully as possible so that the eggs will not lose volume.

Immediately pour batter into prepared cake pans and bake 30 to 35 minutes. When done, the cakes will be golden brown and will spring back when pressed lightly in the center. Let cool in pans 5 minutes, then turn out onto a rack to cool completely.

Frost top of one layer with some of the Coffee Butter Cream. Place second layer on top and completely frost top and sides of cake with remaining Coffee Butter Cream.

If you like, mark the milestone with a circle of small chocolate cups placed atop the cake; fill with a cordial and propose a toast with each portion.

COFFEE BUTTER CREAM

⅔ cup sugar
¼ cup water
5 egg yolks
1 cup butter, softened
2 tablespoons instant coffee powder
2 teaspoons hot water

Dissolve sugar in water over moderate heat. Raise heat and boil until syrup reaches 238° on a candy thermometer — the soft ball stage.

Beat egg yolks lightly. Pour in the hot sugar syrup in a thin stream, beating constantly. When all sugar has been added, continue to beat until the mixture is cool, about 5 minutes more. It should be light and thick.

Add softened butter a little at a time, beating in each addition thoroughly before adding more. Dissolve instant coffee in hot water; add to the butter cream, beating just until incorporated.

About 2 cups.

SPECIAL CHAMPAGNE PUNCH

1 cup unsweetened pineapple juice
¼ cup sugar
½ cup vodka
¼ cup brandy
  Juice of ½ lemon
1 bottle (24 ounces) champagne, well chilled
  Fresh strawberries or orange slices

Combine pineapple juice, sugar, vodka, brandy and lemon juice in a glass bowl or jar, stirring to dissolve sugar. Cover and refrigerate several hours or overnight to mellow.

Just before serving, pour over ice cubes or an ice ring in a punch bowl. Add chilled champagne and stir gently. Garnish with fresh whole strawberries or orange slices.

10 servings (4 ounces each).

INDEX